Kagawa

OF JAPAN

CYRIL J. DAVEY

Kagawa

OF JAPAN

ABINGDON PRESS

NEW YORK . NASHVILLE

JB
KAG

SET IN MONOTYPE GARAMOND AND PRINTED IN
GREAT BRITAIN BY THE CAMELOT PRESS LTD
LONDON AND SOUTHAMPTON

Preface

LIKE SO MANY others, my first introduction to Dr
Toyohiko Kagawa was in the early 1930's. I read William
Axling's *Kagawa*, published by the SCM Press, and it made
an impression on me which I shall never forget. It seemed
as if St Francis of Assisi had come to life again in the slums
of Japan. In the years that followed, especially during the
war, I wondered what had happened to him, but news was
scanty and often contradictory. When I was asked a year
ago to write an *Eagle Book* for boys and girls, for the
Edinburgh House Press, I found it was really extremely
difficult to piece the story together. The chronology was
not easy to work out at times, and material was surprisingly scanty in Britain. No 'Life' had been published here
since Axling's book and, though two had been published
in America since the war, one was out of print (I have not
yet been able to get hold of a copy) and the other dealt
with the period from 1939 to 1959 in a dozen pages. It
was clear that there was need for someone to retell his
story, assess his contribution to the Christian Church, and
to fill the gap of these more or less hidden years during
which, in fact, he was so active. It would have been quite
impossible to do this had it not been for the assistance of
a number of friends, and I very gratefully acknowledge
my indebtedness to them.

Miss Barbara Sullivan, General Editor of Edinburgh
House Press, must head the list. She not only bombarded
me with suggestions and cuttings but, better still, put me
in touch with Dr C. J. R. Bates of Toronto. Dr Bates,

v

a personal friend of Kagawa from the early days, sent books, magazines, papers and personal reminiscences, some of great personal value, across the Atlantic. This book could not have been written without them. His son-in-law, the Rev. Claude de Maestral, of the International Missionary Council, was also most kind in lending material. The Rev. Dr Omiya of Tokyo, at the request of a mutual friend, Mr Hayami, provided me with detailed information about Dr Kagawa's movements and work during and after the war. This was quite invaluable.

With three exceptions, the poems are all reprinted from *Songs From the Slums*, published by the Student Christian Movement Press. 'The Cross the Whole of Christ' (page 88) is from *Meditations on the Cross*, also published by SCM Press. 'Tears' (page 106) is from *Poems for Life*, published by Willett, Clark & Co. Ltd, and 'The Kingdom of God is Within You' (page 129) from *Poems from the Land of Dawn*, published by Friendship Press Inc.

I am most grateful to the publishers concerned, and to Dr Kagawa himself, for permission to include these poems which lay open to us so much of the author's mind and spirit.

CYRIL J. DAVEY

EPSOM, SURREY
1959

Contents

CHAPTER ONE

The Lonely Boy

THE LITTLE, dark-haired child was born in the Year of the Rat, the twenty-first of the Emperor Meiji's reign. It was a good time to be born, said the wise old women who attended at the birth, for the rat symbolized plenty. As the vermin found plenty of grain, so would the child's years be filled with riches, honour and prosperity, until at last he reached a comfortable old age in the great house his father's wealth guaranteed. They nodded their shaven heads, smiled down with their blackened teeth at the *geisha* who was the boy's mother, and went out chattering. They could not know that, though he would live long and be honoured throughout the world, his fame would have nothing to do with riches. Nor could any astrologer have guessed or dared to prophesy that the swiftly-emerging power of Japan would both grasp at the whole of south-east Asia and crumble in ruins before the child was sixty years old.

Every forward-looking citizen of Japan would have said it was a good time to be born, as did the old women. The age-old isolation of these eastern islands, like that of the mainland of China, was passing swiftly away. For centuries Japan had been a closed and mysterious land, living its own life of beauty and tradition. Its emperor had been secluded, as was natural in the descendant of the Sun-god. Its real rulers had been the *samurai*, the warriors with their great burnished swords, and the Buddhist priests. Every village had its temple, to which the simple peasants went

I

devoutly, consoled for their desperate poverty with the knowledge that suffering and hunger were their fate, to be accepted without anger or argument. The day would come when, after endless re-births, they would cease to suffer and cease to exist. Every group of villages, too, had its overlord, a warrior ruler to whom they owed absolute obedience. Within these traditional limits the villagers had been content, their stoical acceptance of the burden of life unchallenged by new ideas of religion, economics or Western civilization. Despite their poverty, they were a cheerful and often gay people, with a love of beauty which has left to the world delicate carvings, charming pictures and lacquer-work, and the exquisite conception of miniature gardens still to be found in town and village.

In 1888 Japan was no longer isolated. Half a dozen American ships, before the middle of the century, had tried to make some kind of trade agreement without success, but in 1854 Commodore Perry came, and managed to negotiate a treaty between the United States and Japan. From that time forward the East lost some of its mystery and Japan began to find her place in the modern world. Swiftly taking up the slack of the lost centuries, she hauled quickly into the wake of the great trading nations. Before long, her commercial leaders were determined to overtake and even pass them. The Japanese people showed almost at once that, whether they had gifts of leadership or not, they certainly had ability to copy and adapt what they saw in America. Britain was a long way off. For many years the United States were to be the teachers and, later, the uneasy rivals of Japanese commerce and industry. It was undoubtedly an exciting time to be born.

Across the country went the telegraph wires. Railways were built. Newspapers began to be published. Schools were established. Students went to America and Europe, and came back to help build and man the new factories which were growing up in the rapidly-extending cities. In the West there was a fashion for things Japanese. Scroll paintings, lacquer work, parasols and Japanese lanterns were part of this new fashion, and in the more serious world of art, painters like Whistler and musicians like Puccini, with his *Madam Butterfly*, helped to make the Japanese way of thought more familiar—to say nothing of Sullivan and *The Mikado*, which illustrates both the interest and the ignorance of the West about Japan. The impact of Western culture began to break down traditional habits even in the country districts. The poor no longer took off their wooden clogs as they bowed to the rich, nor did horsemen dismount to walk by the residence of their wealthy landlord.

Kobe, one of the great towns of the twentieth century, grew from a huddle of small fishing-villages into a port where not only the vessels of other nations but the shipping companies of Japan itself were found in large numbers. The owner of one of these companies was a wealthy and important nobleman called Denjiro Kagawa. He was a man with a strange, but not unusual, history.

Denjiro Isobe belonged to an ancient, aristocratic family, linked with the rulers of the land and descended from the great *samurai*. He was, however, the third son and, as such, had little chance of inheriting more than an honourable name. The Kagawa family had daughters, but no son. Marriages were always 'arranged' in Japan and, when Denjiro was fifteen and Michi Kagawa was eight, they were betrothed, by consent of both families. To ensure the proper succession from father to son, Denjiro was adopted by the Kagawas, as well as betrothed to their daughter, and given their family name. After their marriage, the young people went to live in the family 'mansion', a large typical farmhouse at Awa, on the island of Shikoku across the bay from Kobe, and on the death of Michi's father, Denjiro Kagawa came into control of the family fortune.

He was a man of ability as well as wealth. In the province of Awa, he was the headman of nineteen villages, but this local eminence did not satisfy his ambition or his talents. He became associated with the governing group in the country and was appointed Secretary to the Privy Council, the committee of privileged men who had access to the Emperor and acted as his advisers. He himself had the standing of a cabinet minister. His main interests, however, were not political. He had a hard-driving energy and, evidently, considerable business acumen, for he used the Kagawa fortune to become a pioneer in the new commercial ventures. He had interests in the railways, but seeing the prospects in international trade, he helped to found and became the owner of one of Kobe's principal shipping companies.

All these activities involved his spending more and more time in Kobe, Tokyo and the other big cities. The family farmhouse, in a country backwater, had no interest for him. Nor had the wife he married as a youth. If he was a man of his time so far as his commercial interests were concerned, so he was in character and behaviour. He has been dismissed by writers as sensual, dissolute, unprincipled and callous. So he may have been, but in this he was typical of many of his class. It is true that he left his wife and her ill-tempered mother to care for the farm and seldom went back to Awa. Instead, he chose to live with a *geisha* in Kobe. This, too, was not unusual, and it is unfair to judge his action by Christian standards. As one of the richest magnates of Japan, he would have found it hard to see why he should not do as he wished, so long as Michi was provided for on the farm.

Though Denjiro left his legal wife he was comparatively

faithful to Kame, the *geisha* with whom he lived for most of his adult life. They had five children. The oldest was a son, Tan-Ichi, who grew up to inherit his father's moral attitude to life without his ability. The next was a girl, Ei, a strange, weepy unbalanced child. The third, born fifteen years after his older brother, was a boy, and there were two still younger.

Toyohiko Kagawa, the second son, was born on 10th July 1888. When he was seven days old he was given his first name, at a family festival. His father was loyal enough to old traditions to call him after Toyouke daijin, the god of O-Asahiko shrine not far from his ancestral home. On his thirty-first day, dressed in a tiny black *kimono*, he was carried to the nearby shrine to be blessed by the Shinto priest. When he was a hundred and twenty days old there was another celebration. In another new *kimono*, embroidered with the family crest—even the poorest families had their own crest—he was the centre of a third feast, when a lacquer tray filled with delicacies was placed in front of him and he was given a single grain of rice, his first solid food.

'*Omedeto*', said the relatives and friends, bowing before the baby and wishing him luck, giving him papiermâché dogs so that he might grow as fast and fat as a young puppy, before they retired to their own feast of rice and red beans. Until he was three years old he was carried on his mother's or his sister's back, and only then was he taken to the shrine once more to be blessed as he passed from babyhood to boyhood. Few children could have been happier. It was a wealthy home, though it was furnished with the usual Japanese graceful simplicity. Denjiro was proud of his family and, to secure the boys in their proper inheritance, he adopted Tan-Ichi and Toyohiko as his legal sons. Kame, his mother, always remained in Toyohiko's mind as the gentlest and most beautiful woman he could remember. If he gained some of his energy and his interest in 'schemes' from his father, there is little doubt that he inherited his gentle, sensitive nature from his mother and that it was transformed, first through his youthful loneliness and then through his Christian experience, into profound compassion. Although, as a Christian reformer, he rebelled against the moral standards which his home symbolized, his character derived in no small part from his early years and from his parents.

It was just a year after the ceremony in which he was accepted as a full-grown boy that tragedy swept over the Kagawa household. Toyohiko was playing outside the house. More precisely, he was quarrelling with another small boy and had just picked up a wooden bar from the door to reinforce his argument, when his father's clerk came out of the house. Toyohiko knew his father was ill, but that was all. Now, as he followed the servant into the bedroom, the little boy felt the beginnings of the loneliness which was to haunt him for the next few years. The room seemed very full of grown-ups, who made way for him to approach his father. They were very quiet, but not so still as his father. A medal of honour, sent by the Turkish Government, lay by his side. It had come that same morning, but the sick man was too frail to hold it— too ill to speak to his family or even, perhaps, recognize them. A little while later he died.

Toyohiko did not realize for some time—not, indeed, until his foster-mother kept on pointing it out to him when he went to live at Awa—that his father had died as the result of his self-indulgence and dissipation. Later, when he saw the same process repeating itself in his brother, he had to accept the truth. On the other hand, he could never really bring himself to regard his mother, Kame, the *geisha*, as an immoral or dissolute woman. She belonged to a class of women who were not merely decorative playthings for men with money to spend, but were highly trained in the courtesies and domestic arts of traditional Japanese society. Kame, indeed, had been for more than twenty-five years the faithful wife of Denjiro Kagawa in the eyes of everyone except the women of his own legal household. There was nothing surprising or, to many, shameful in the relationship. Toyohiko had known nothing but the Kobe home, and for him and the younger children his mother was the centre of his love and his life. His father's death surprised him. Then the funeral was over, with all its ceremonies and strange excitements, and the household settled down once more. The candles in the household shrine were kept alight; offerings of food were set out there and the smell of incense hung about the room. This was as it should be, for the spirits of dead ancestors hovered about the shrine. A Buddhist child accepted these things naturally and found nothing frightening in death.

Two months later the real tragedy happened. Kame fell ill and died as suddenly as her husband had done. Death, this time, was unbearable. The voices of the priests, chanting their melancholy liturgy, frightened him.

> *Transient are all.*
> *All being born must die.*
> *Being born, they are dead already.*
> *Being dead, they are glad to be at rest.*

The neighbours consulted with Tan-Ichi, now in his twenties, and with Denjiro's relatives, and plans were made. Though they concerned the little boy, the arguments merely went on round him and over his head until everything was ready. He was desperately miserable and found no comfort anywhere in his dissolving world, except now and

7

again in his big brother's arms. The Kobe house was sold and its furniture disposed of. The two younger children were taken away. Tan-Ichi explained to his brother and sister that he would be staying in Kobe, but that they would be taken to their father's proper home at Awa to live with his real wife and her mother. There would be no reason to worry about money. The Kagawa fortunes were large, despite all that Denjiro had spent, and even if anything happened to the shipping company there would still be the farm at Awa to keep the family going.

Toyohiko hardly listened, for most of it was incomprehensible to a four-year-old child. All he knew was that he was going away from Kobe and the home where he had been happy to a strange island over the bay to live with a woman his father had married but had not loved. She would not be like his mother, thought little Toyohiko —beautiful and kind. She would probably be horrible and cruel. There would be no other children to play with, and after the excitements of the city he did not want to live in the country. He did not want to live anywhere. He looked at his weeping sister. Ei was queer, he said to himself, and would be no sort of company. Every vestige of security had left him. He wished that, like his mother, he could die. This morbid sense of insecurity was to haunt him for more than ten years.

It was to be expected that Toyohiko and Ei would be unwelcome. They represented to Michi Kagawa and her mother all the years of infidelity and unhappiness that had followed Denjiro's marriage. While Denjiro had climbed to power, becoming one of the wealthiest men in Japan, the two women had managed the family farm, working hard and bickering for twenty-five years or so, putting up resentfully with their narrow existence. The stories which reached them from Kobe did not make their life any more bearable. It was not surprising that, from the beginning, Toyohiko's life was made miserable. Michi seems to have accepted him more readily than her mother. The old woman was determined to make the little boy pay for his father's infidelity.

The ancestral farmhouse at Awa was a sprawling and typical Japanese manor, as different from the neat home in Kobe as the flat countryside was from the busy wharves of the town itself. It seemed to sprawl in every direction, one room opening through the tissue-paper doors into another, giving fascinating glimpses of the farmyard through the lattice windows, until the rooms gave place to dark passages leading to dusty, cluttered cupboards and outhouses. The floors were covered with soft straw mats, constantly needing renewal, so that from the beginning there was always work for poor Ei to do. In the great thatched roof, birds and tiny animals could be heard thrusting their way towards their nests.

Outside, at the rear of the house, was a garden filled with dwarf trees, stone lanterns and carved beasts, shaded by red maples and giant pines. Beyond lay the bamboo grove and the indigo and, beyond that again, the sugar cane and the flat plains of the rice-fields. The farmhouse was five miles from the sea, but a short distance away ran the Yoshino river, with sand-dunes bordering it. A mile away, across the fields, rose the moated mausoleum of an ancient and forgotten emperor.

Toyohiko, treated with respect by his father's servants and pampered by his mother, was thrust suddenly into a world where he was bullied, half-starved and made to work like a little slave. Possibly he did not have to toil harder than any other boy who grew up on a busy Japanese farm, but his memories made the contrast particularly bitter, and the enmity of his grandmother had no place for thanks or endearments. Certainly the work never ceased. The rice had to be harvested with sickles, and the straw carried on his back. The water-wheel was worked by treading endlessly up the revolving steps. Mulberry leaves must be picked for the silk-worms. Bamboo-canes had to be cut. In the winter, there were sandals and mats to be made from the rice-straw, radishes and other root-vegetables to be pickled, silk and cotton to be spun.

It is easy to read into his misery a worse situation than really existed. Children are seldom physically ill-treated in Japan, and though he had to carry heavier loads in the fields and work harder on the farm than was reasonable for any small boy, his suffering lay within. He was unloved and unwanted, and to a sensitive child with Toyohiko's early upbringing this was almost unbearable. There was no one to whom he could turn, except on the occasions when his big brother came to the farm. His sister was becoming an invalid, and to the villagers who worked on the farm he was an object of scorn and suspicion, a town-bred child whom their parents talked about with contempt. This loneliness and isolation were the worst part of his life, and they would have been unbearable had it not been for the comfort he found in the world of nature and, a little later, in books.

Shunned by those of his own age, he found his peculiar consolations. They were those of a child who by nature or circumstances was a solitary. He roamed the countryside on his own, exulting in the butterflies, dragonflies and the brilliantly-coloured little birds which skimmed over the fields and the river. He spent time fishing, or wandering round the mausoleum and putting down nets in the moat. Often he sought refuge in the bamboo grove, or in making a miniature garden of his own. To the astonishment of the women and the servants, he would shut himself up for hours in the store-house where the family possessions and heirlooms were kept. They believed it to be haunted by the spirits of long-dead ancestors and would not go near it, but to Toyohiko, with its boxes of traditional costumes, rusting armour and *samurai* swords, it was a treasury of endless delight and discovery. More precious than anything else were the old scrolls and books which he pulled out from corners and cupboards.

Despite all the work he had to do on the farm, he was sent to school earlier than was usual, a year before most other children in the village. Education was simple enough in the little primary school, but Toyohiko was a naturally quick and alert child, and the reading he did in school was supplemented later on by the Chinese classics he discovered in the family treasure-room. As the years passed, he moved swiftly to the top of the school, and the more he learned, the more he longed for still more learning. It was clear that he could never be satisfied within the limits of the village and the farm.

Religion, of course, formed the main part of the school curriculum. The children learned the Confucian classics, with their emphasis on filial piety and patriotism as the two dominant virtues. The latter was, to the Japanese, of immense importance. The Emperor not only represented the deity but was, in some sense, a deity himself. Japan was expanding its trade, building up its industries, and, to add to its markets and its self-esteem, had temporarily gone to war with China. It must have been already evident, even to a small boy, that any criticism of his own country and its system was regarded not merely as disloyalty but treachery. The Confucian system was concerned with behaviour, rather than religious belief. Buddhism was the common faith, and here, too, it was made plain that to forsake one's ancestral religion for another was unthinkable to a loyal Japanese. Though Christian missionaries were at work in the towns, they had made very little headway in the country districts.

Toyohiko, as he grew older, began to take his place as the one male member of the Kagawa family resident in the district. In the celebrations at the Buddhist temple he had, to his childish embarrassment, to accept the seat of honour due to his rank and position. The contrast between loneliness and honour, dislike of his parentage and respect for his abilities, did nothing to give him peace or self-confidence. He had lost the bitterness of his first days at Awa, when he would gladly have thrown himself into the Yoshino river and been swept away to sea, but he still felt acutely miserable and unwanted. The village children, losing nothing of their scorn for him as they grew older, added to this a violent jealousy for his educational brilliance. They could not ill-treat him. His position put him beyond that. On one occasion, however, they tried, successfully enough, to blame him for a serious accident.

The daughter of the school caretaker was carried home badly hurt, and the children accused Toyohiko of having knocked her over and pushed her into the ditch. He could not defend himself, for they had ganged up against him and denied everything he said. Only later was it admitted that the girl had fallen from the water-wheel and hurt herself by accident. Village opinion turned sharply against Toyohiko when there seemed some chance that the child would die. Unable to prove his innocence, he took the little money he had managed to save, bought gifts of fruit and sweets and took them to her house. When she did die he was unable to console himself, feeling as though in some mysterious way he had, in fact, been the cause of everything after all.

In despair, Toyohiko told the story to his brother when he came to stay at the farm. He was only ten years old, a year too young to leave the primary school, but he managed to persuade Tan-Ichi to intercede with his grandmother, the real ruler of the household, to allow him to go to the Middle School in the town. To his surprise, the women agreed. After six years at Awa, Toyohiko took his last walks through the familiar fields and bazaars. The kites swept overhead, the dragonflies darted above the river, and the frogs croaked in the muddy water. A new unease swept over him. He had been lonely, certainly, but he found joy in these familiar sights and sounds. He walked down the bazaar that he knew so well, looking at the model forts and soldiers being sold in the shops to celebrate Japan's victory over China, and knew he was going to miss everything more than he had thought.

The day for his departure came at last, and even his grandmother was more tender than usual. Accompanied by the fashionably dressed Tan-Ichi, he set out once more across the bay. Six years ago he had come, a frightened little boy, from Kobe. Now, as he started off for Toku-shima, he knew that for the second time in his life security had slipped away.

CHAPTER TWO

'Make me like Christ'

THE MOOD OF uncertainty, a mixture of excited discovery and despondent failure, was to be with young Kagawa throughout his schooldays and the two college courses which followed. At the same time, after a year or so at the Middle School in Tokushima, he was to be driven by an increasing sense of purpose, though not for another ten years was that purpose to become clear either to himself or to those who knew him. Then, from that Christmas Day in 1909, when he was twenty-one years old, it was to hold him inexorably until it began to change the thinking of the Church and the pattern of Japanese life itself.

The ferry-boat, a long ride by jinricksha, followed by a dusty walk into the town of Tokushima itself, left him frightened and lonely. The examination which followed was equally terrifying to a ten-year-old boy. All he had gained so far was permission to sit the entrance examination to the Tokushima Middle School. Neither his brother's wealth nor his uncle's eminence could guarantee that he would be admitted. He was, after all, a year younger than the other candidates, and less than half of those who sat would pass. It was astonishing to him when he found his name on the notice-board amongst the successful boys.

For a sensitive child, the months that followed were both harsh and exciting. He found the boys in the dormitory crude, ill-mannered and unpleasant. The older students

14

boasted freely about their drinking and their sexual adventures. There was a good deal of homosexuality. Toyohiko was revolted and appalled. Years later he wrote: 'I longed that the ship of life would suddenly sink, and I could go down with it in peace.' At the same time he was entering a new world of thought, in which both teachers and books played a full part. He was a good scholar, eager to learn all he could, dreaming of the days when he too would be a man of importance—a teacher or professor, or even, like the father he could hardly remember, a member of the Government.

It was soon apparent that, if he were to achieve anything in the new world which Japan had entered, he must learn English. A number of other boys had the same idea, and it was through this that he made his first contact with Christian missionaries. He had no intention of inquiring about their religion, much less of becoming a Christian, though one of the teachers at the Middle School, Mr Katayama, was a Christian, and he heard that some of the older students were accepting the Western faith. Toyohiko was a staunch Buddhist, like all his family, and his only sight of a Christian book had been of the Gospel of Matthew. Never having heard the name before and misconstruing the Japanese characters, he was amused at the stupidity of religious people who devoutly read 'the book about making horses grow bigger'! Foolish though they might be, however, the missionaries spoke English, and he joined the group of eager boys who went to the homes of Dr Harry Myers, a Presbyterian minister, and his brother-in-law, Dr Logan, to learn the language which would open the way to success. The missionaries, like most of those in Japan at this time, were Americans.

Slowly he began to find his way amongst the strange sounds and letters. The early plodding gave way to swift enthusiasm, and before long he was asking for books to read. Dr Myers lent him a New Testament, and he needed no urging to try to read it. In the Gospel of Luke, with which he began, he found a Man who lived close to nature but loved men, especially the unhappy ones, still more than He did the lilies and the birds. The ethical teaching of the Gospel made little impression on him. It was the character of Jesus which caught hold of his imagination. When Myers went on holiday, he left his English class with instructions to memorize certain passages in the Sermon on the Mount. Toyohiko did more. He read and re-read the whole section. Even so, he did not reach the end of the story. English was still a foreign language.

Just about this time, tragedy overwhelmed him once more. His older brother, Tan-Ichi, had agreed to pay his school-fees. That was why it was possible to leave Awa and come to Tokushima. Tan-Ichi's responsibility went no farther, however. He had no interest in Toyohiko's progress. Indeed, as the younger boy soon discovered, it was not easy even to make him produce the money for the fees. Toyohiko had childish memories of the house in Kobe where he had grown up—of discreet luxury, smoothly sliding doors and papiermâché windows. To his astonishment, when he first saw it, Tan-Ichi's house had a splendour that was far greater. It was bigger than the old home in Kobe, its furnishings were more flamboyant, and in place of paper, the doors and windows were panelled with real glass. Tan-Ichi, however, was not often to be found there, though the women who lived with him, with their thickly-powdered faces and high-piled black hair, could be heard chattering shrilly beyond the doors. Wearily young Toyohiko made his way from one exclusive restaurant to another, until he found his brother, half-drunk, attended by two or three *geishas* who giggled while Tan-Ichi fumbled with his money and passed over the few coins needed to keep the boy at school for another month.

Then, quite suddenly, Tan-Ichi died. That seemed bad enough. Despite his way of living, he was the only person for whom Toyohiko really cared deeply. The next news was far worse. Tan-Ichi was far more profligate than his father had been. He had squandered the whole of the family fortunes. Not only so, he had pledged the family property. There was literally nothing left to live on. Even the farmhouse at Awa, belonging to the family for generations, was seized by Tan-Ichi's creditors. All that was left —and this was by their generosity—was a *go-down*, a building about the size of an ordinary room, into which the three women, Michi, her step-mother, and the invalid Ei, had to squeeze themselves and their few personal belongings. The school-fees stopped, too.

Denjiro Kagawa's older brother, Toyohiko's uncle, had inherited the Isobe fortunes and kept the family name. He was president of the railway and shipping company, and with typical Japanese family solidarity he undertook to continue Toyohiko's schooling, but instead of maintaining him as a boarder, he took him into his own household. So that he might earn his fees, he made him tutor to his two young sons, with one of whom he shared a study bedroom.

These fresh troubles and changes drove Toyohiko into a new state of despondency. Despite his instinctive revulsion against sensuality and luxury, he wondered if there were not an inherent family tendency which would bring him to the same life and the same end. It was at just this period of sensitivity that he heard Dr Myers tell the end of the Gospel story. The Japanese cry easily when they are moved, and the tears would not be held back as he listened to the account of the crucifixion.

'Is this true?' he asked Myers later.

The missionary nodded. 'Quite true.'

'Jesus died?' Toyohiko could not believe it. 'He was killed, after everything he had done for people, after all the kindness he had shown them?'

Myers looked at the stricken boy. 'He died because he loved them,' he answered quietly.

Before he left the missionary's study that evening, Toyohiko Kagawa knelt on the mat and made his first Christian prayer.

'Oh God, make me like Christ!', he asked, simply.

Now the New Testament became a new book. There was no slackening of his school-work; indeed, he worked harder than ever. But the despair had lifted. He knew that he would not go the way of his father and his brother. A new power was open to him. Life had become an opportunity to live like Christ. In spite of this, he made no profession of his new faith, either at home or in school. He knew what had happened to some of the young rebels and liberals, older than himself, who had been baptized as Christians.

One day Myers questioned him quite directly. 'Do you say your prayers?'

'Yes.'

'Where?'

'Under the bed-clothes, before I go to sleep.'

Myers raised his eyebrows, though he was not surprised. Toyohiko belonged to a wealthy, traditional Buddhist household. Every morning he was expected to come downstairs and join his uncle and his cousins in meditation before the Buddhist shrine. True, he could turn his mind to Jesus instead of Buddha, but outwardly he must conform if there was to be any security left.

'Ought you not to be baptized?'

It was the question Toyohiko knew must come sooner or later, the question he had refused even to put to himself. 'No,' he replied. 'If I did my family would disown me.'

'What then?'

'Well——' He shuffled uncomfortably. 'I should be unable to come to school any more.'

Myers looked at him until the boy finally raised his eyes. 'So you are a coward?'

It was not a taunt. Toyohiko took it as it was meant, a plain statement of fact. It was the truth, and the only answer lay in action. At the age of fifteen he was baptized as a Christian.

The result, at home, was not what he expected. Old Isobe, his uncle, shrugged his shoulders. Not a few young men were becoming Christians. It seemed to be part of the price Japan must pay for progress in the race with the West. Religion, in any case, was not as important as all that. Prosperity mattered most, the sort of prosperity that would make it possible for Japan to wage war successfully against her neighbours—and win. Toyohiko was allowed to stay on in the Isobe household and continue his studies at school. It was at school, indeed, rather than at home, that the first test of his new faith occurred.

A few years earlier Japan had made war successfully against China. Now it was evident that if she were to keep her place in the modern world she would have to face war once more. Russian forces had occupied Manchuria and pressed on into North Korea. Once that was occupied, it was feared that the Tsar would try to conquer Japan. Forestalling such a move, the Japanese Government declared war on Russia. This time it was not to prove as easy as the fight against untrained Chinese peasants. Port Arthur, where the Russian fleet was anchored, was finally taken, but only after six months' fighting in which twenty thousand Japanese soldiers fell. It was typical of the campaigns that followed. Men were conscripted into the army and boys too young to go to war were drilled in the schools.

Toyohiko heard again and again in his mind the words of Jesus, demanding love for one's enemies, and saw Him dying on the Cross rather than resist those who hated Him. With the rest of the school he was led out on to the athletics field, now turned into a parade ground. He stretched out his hand and took the gun which the teacher thrust at him. Then, suddenly, he flung it down.

'Kagawa! Pick up your gun!'

Toyohiko neither moved nor replied. The crowd went tense, and the instructor's face twisted with anger.

'Why do you not do what I order?'

In the silence Toyohiko's reply was audible across the field. 'Because I believe Japan is wrong to go to war!'

A moment later he lay on the ground, squirming as the infuriated teacher who had knocked him down went on kicking him in the face and stomach. When the attack was over, he dragged himself to his feet and stumbled from the field.

Toyohiko's act of pacifism won him respect while it lost him some friends. It was the first completely individual stand he had made, and it marked him out even more than his academic brilliance as a boy of character. To Myers and Logan, up to this point, he had been a quiet, thoughtful, sincere lad, willing to face ignominy for the sake of his new faith. They now realized that he was much more than this, and began to look on him as a potential leader. In the two years which followed his baptism, Myers became his *Sensei*—an untranslatable word which includes the spiritual authority of the Indian *guru* and the intimacy of deep friendship. They talked of spiritual matters, debated theology and philosophy, discussed politics, war and industrialism. From the school library, under the supervision of Myers, Toyohiko borrowed book after book, including the American Thoreau and the Russian Tolstoi. Both gave stronger form to his growing pacifism.

One day he accompanied Myers on one of the missionary's regular visits to the filthy slums of Tokushima. It was an area to which the respectable citizens closed their eyes, where lived the beggars, thieves and outcasts of the city. Wandering through the narrow, evil-smelling alleys, Myers led him to a tiny hut. Here, amidst all the dirt and degradation, they were welcomed by a young man who, despite his emaciation and evident illness, had a strangely happy face. Toyohiko listened to his story with amazement.

Growing up in Osaka, he had stolen five yen from a timber-merchant. To escape the police, he had run away to Tokyo and there he had been arrested in a very different fashion. Passing a preaching-place, he had gone in to see what was going on and been converted. He became an honest labourer, and when he earned five yen, took it back to the timber-merchant to repay what he had stolen. Then, on the outbreak of the Russo-Japanese war, he had enlisted in the 43rd Regiment. From the battles in which his unit had been engaged, only four men came back alive. While he was in the army he had saved money from his pay and sent it back to some of the beggars he knew in the slums of Tokushima. Now, discharged from service because he was unfit to fight, he had come home—to live in the slums, not from compulsion but from choice, to serve the degraded as he felt Christ Himself would have done.

Only a few years later, Toyohiko used the story as the basis of his novel, *A Grain of Wheat*, renaming the young man Ichii, and making him the hero of his story. The ex-soldier-turned-preacher, however, was to have a more important effect on his life than merely providing him with the theme of a novel.

By the time he was seventeen, Toyohiko's mind was clear as he looked into the future. His Uncle Isobe, proud of his nephew's academic progress, hoping to retrieve the family honour, urged him to go to the Imperial University in Tokyo. He would himself meet all the costs. At the end of his stay there, even if there were no place for him in the railway and shipping businesses, he might well move into politics and become a leader in the Government. The old man's assessment of Toyohiko's abilities was shrewd enough. There were to be days in the future when the Prime Minister, and even the Emperor, would urge him to take his place in the Cabinet. But those days were far off. Toyohiko knew what he wanted to be.

'No, sir,' he answered, deliberately but with deference. 'I have no wish to go to Tokyo. I intend to be a Christian minister.'

Isobe might tolerate his nephew's changing his faith, but this was another matter altogether. Persuasion and protest were both useless. Angrily he laid down an ultimatum. A day or so later, Toyohiko packed a few clothes and left the Isobe household, disinherited and, in his uncle's eyes, disgraced. Once more he was without security, but this time he had his Christian faith.

CHAPTER THREE

Toyohiko Changes His Mind

THERE WAS ONLY one place to which Toyohiko could go. Carrying his small bundle of clothes, he made his way to Myers's house and told him what had happened. It was no surprise to the missionary. Indeed, the only puzzling aspect of the matter was that it had not happened before. Clearly, old Uncle Isobe had hoped that Toyohiko would bring honour to the family name. Instead, he was determined to disgrace it, turning his back on the old loyalties, joining the little group of rebels and extremists who followed a foreign religion and would no doubt turn into traitors if there were any conflict between their own country and the West. It was surprising, the shipping magnate had taunted his nephew, that he did not side with the Russians. Then, recalling Toyohiko's criticism of the war which was still raging, he had lost his temper once again. The missionaries could imagine the angry old man as Toyohiko told them of the last interview. Indeed, they lived so close to the Japanese people that they had some sympathy for his disappointment. Their sympathy for Toyohiko, however, went deeper. After a brief consultation they decided that he must be sent on to the Mission's 'continuation school', the Presbyterian College in Tokyo, and that funds must be found to make it possible. Accepting the support of the Mission, as he had had to accept that of his brother and his uncle, Toyohiko gladly agreed. At the age of seventeen, more fully prepared than he had been for either of his previous changes of life, he set off for the capital.

Tokyo may have seemed strange, with its large buildings and busy thoroughfares, but it was a familiar, Japanese strangeness. The college library, on the other hand, was utterly foreign and bizarre, built in imitation of an English manor-house, with mullioned windows, dark beams, and sharply pointed turrets and archways. Yet it was here, amongst the ten thousand books which lined the long shelves, that Toyohiko felt most at home. Books were always sure company. He made up his mind to take one down and read it through every day before he went to sleep. Tremendous though the task was, it was a resolution he more or less managed to carry out.

Dr Myers had already done a great deal to develop Toyohiko's interest in books, particularly in the field of theology and philosophy. Kant, Darwin, Ruskin, Max Muller's *Sacred Books of the East*, would be strong meat even for the digestion of a Western seventeen-year-old going to a university. Toyohiko, to whom English had been an unknown language five years earlier, had already delved into some of them, and began to study the rest with the ease and gusto which most young people bring to an adventure story. It was evident that his mind was far above average, his memory excellent and his interests unusual. From theology and philosophy he widened his concern to include the other difficult fields of sociology and economics.

To professors and fellow-students, however, he appeared queer, isolated, unduly high-minded and often inattentive —this last because he had already mastered what was being taught, or had been awake until dawn reading a volume from the library. Individualists are seldom popular, and the causes they champion have, when they take them up, little public support. This was particularly true of Toyohiko's pacifism and his concern for the unprivileged. The war with Russia was still continuing to drain Japan's resources of men and material, and Toyohiko was more firmly entrenched in his opinions about it. Now, however, with his wide reading, he argued in the college debating-society against war as an institution, rather than against the struggle going on at that moment. He came down firmly against the almost united opposition of the whole college, on the side of Christian pacifism. These opinions might have been tolerated as no more than studentish whims and debating points if he had not, on being challenged, gone on to attack his own Government's international policy.

One evening he was summoned to the athletics field. Wondering why anyone would want to see him there at that time of the day, he followed the student who had come to fetch him. Immediately he was off the main path, a group of young men gathered at the side of the field surged towards him, their faces set and their fists clenched. Before he realized what was happening he was knocked down.

'Traitor!'

'Dirty Russian!'

'Enemy of the people!' they yelled, as they beat him down, punching and kicking him where he lay. 'This will knock your pacifism out of you!' Then, panting from the excitement of their savage attack, they stood aside, waiting to jeer as he crawled away.

The descendant of the *samurai*, whose ancestors never forgave an injury, rose slowly—not to his feet, but to his knees. His trembling hands were clasped together, and his attackers listened silently to the high-pitched voice.

'Father, forgive them. They know not what they do.'

One by one, shamed by a pacifism that had its springs in love, they turned away and slunk off the field. None of them helped Toyohiko to his feet; none of them looked at him or at each other. They knew that he was a man

C

apart from themselves. Amongst those who walked awkwardly from the field that evening was one who, later on, as a minister, was to share in Kagawa's ordination.

Toyohiko had little money, and what he had came from charity, given by missionaries and Christian folk for his support. Even so, he managed to save a little by going without meals. What he saved he gave away to beggars or shared with students poorer than himself. His clothes were shabby, too. Seeing this, the sister of one of the professors made a new cotton *kimono* for him, and then a second one. He wore neither of them, and still went about in his old one and his *hakama*, the wide Japanese trousers tied with a cotton sash. The two *kimonos* were passed on to the cold and hungry children of some of the servants, living in their *go-downs* behind the college.

With a similar feeling he rescued a half-starved kitten and a mangy dog. When his friends expostulated with him, he explained simply: 'Anyone will care for a good-looking, well-fed dog. But who would save this poor mongrel if I didn't?' He spent days looking for the animal when his fellow-students removed it from his room. Anyone or anything in need claimed his compassion. One day, following up a disgusting smell, some of the young men found their way to Toyohiko's room. There, they were appalled to find a scrofulous beggar lying on the sleeping-mat, while Toyohiko knelt at his side and bathed his sores. This was too much for even the college authorities to tolerate. Toyohiko was informed that he might practise his austerities inside the college, but his charity must be exercised outside. He turned once more to books for a while, reading all he could about economics, wages and poverty. Coming across an account of Canon Barnett's work in the London slums, he thought again of the young ex-soldier in Tokushima, and wondered about his future.

There is no doubt that he was a difficult young man, not fitting into the pattern of contemporary Japanese Church life. Indeed, he stopped going to one church because the pastor disapproved of his pacifism, and he stood in the way of a congregation going to another and denounced them for their smug respectability and their disregard of the poor who sat at their gates. Always he could find words in the teaching of Jesus to support what he had to say. His anger with mere churchiness was something that remained with him. 'I reject everything connected with the religions of imposing architecture,' he later wrote. 'It would be well if the world's churches and temples were razed to the ground. Then, perhaps, we might understand what real religion means.'

Nevertheless, even a reformer has his vanity, and Toyohiko coveted a neat, new college uniform worn by many of the young men of his day, dark in colour but livened by white piping round its stiff collar. When Myers sent him some money to buy a set of Plato's works which had caught his eye in a book-shop, he used the money to pay for the uniform. Vanity, however, is no bedfellow for honour. Toyohiko could not sleep with his uneasy conscience. He wrote a long, miserable letter to his *Sensei*, Myers, disappeared from the school for three or four days to think things out, and was never seen in the uniform again. Instead, he chose to wear the cheap simple garments of the poor.

It was about this time that the war with Russia came to an end. President Theodore Roosevelt acted as mediator between the two countries. Japan had won, but when the people, gathered on the streets to cheer the returning heroes, saw the remnant of the army, bedraggled, thin and exhausted, marching under the triumphal arches, their shouts dwindled into silence. When they realized that, under the peace treaty, there would be no reparations, the puzzled silence turned into furious mob-violence. Opponents of the Government used the occasion to turn popular opinion against it. Victory without conquest—both Russia and Japan had had to agree to withdraw from Manchuria— had gone sour in the people's mouths, and demonstrations were held throughout the country. One of them was staged in the theatre of a fishing-village near Kobe. Before long, knives were drawn and murder seemed likely. At that moment, a young man clambered on to the platform and called for silence, and when, a little later, the police arrived to arrest the leaders of the mob, they found the violent men sitting quietly, now and again breaking into applause as Toyohiko Kagawa lectured them about economics and the foolishness of war.

Toyohiko was beginning to feel the power of words, but it was not his main concern at this time to stir up political action. He had determined to be a Christian minister, and he wanted to preach. When his time at the Tokyo College was over he moved back to his birthplace, Kobe, where he intended to spend the next couple of years. A month or two earlier, Myers had written to tell him that a new Theological Seminary was to be opened there, and he had enrolled himself as a student. There was still some time before the term was due to begin, and he became assistant to a pastor in the city, who allowed him to help in preaching and 'open-air work'.

Across the Ikuta river, which ran through Kobe, lay an area into which, like the slums of Tokushima which Toyohiko had visited with Myers, the respectable citizens never penetrated. Nor, for that matter, did the police visit it more than they could help. It was the notorious slum Shinkawa—haunt and refuge of criminals, pimps, vagabonds and murderers, populated largely, though not entirely, by the off-scourings of the towns and villages for many miles around. Toyohiko knew of it. Indeed, everyone knew of it by reputation—and rumour did not paint it worse than it actually was. It was to Shinkawa, however, that the young student, still only nineteen, went with the pastor's encouragement to preach the Gospel of Love. That, indeed, was his only message. Walking day by day across the Higurashi bridge, he found a convenient corner where the disgusting alleyways crossed. There he stood and told any who would listen that God loved them and had sent His Son, Jesus Christ, to make His love known. Hardly anyone listened. Nobody cared when, at the end of forty days, he collapsed and did not come back.

He had been far from well for some time. No one, at his age, could use up energy as he did and not burn himself out. He was carried back from Shinkawa to the pastor's house, and put to bed. For three days his friends thought he would die, and Myers was summoned to be with him in his last hours. Then, as it seemed to his friends and, afterwards, to Toyohiko himself, a miracle occurred. Their prayers were answered and, the crisis past, he began to get better, though the doctor pointed out that he could expect only a partial recovery and a short, restricted life. Like so many millions of Japanese, whether peasants or town-dwellers, he was under-nourished and over-worked. Too little warm clothing and too much exposure to rain and biting winds had aggravated the tendency to 'consumption', as it was then called. He had tuberculosis of the lungs, an almost endemic disease in Japan.

Neither the doctor nor Toyohiko's friends had yet been able to assess the strength of purpose and the spiritual energy which possessed the frail young student. *They* hoped he might get better. *He* knew he must not die. It was impossible that a collapse and a haemorrhage on the other

side of the Higurashi bridge should be his last link with
the slums of Shinkawa. There was too much to do for
him to die. Once off his bed, he quickly gathered enough
strength to go back to his preaching across the river. Again
he collapsed, and this time Myers had him admitted to
hospital. He stayed there for four unhappy, restless months,
at the end of which he had to face the fact that, unless he
were cured, he could not be admitted to the theological
seminary.

Just after the Japanese New Year celebrations, he packed
his few personal belongings once more and set off for the
shores of Atzuma Bay. There, in Gamagori, a poverty-
stricken fishing-village, he found an empty hut and made
his temporary home. Not even the wealthiest Japanese
homes are cluttered with furniture, but Toyohiko's hut was
a strange contrast both to the professors' homes which he
frequented and those of his illiterate fishermen neighbours.
There were a few carefully rolled sleeping-blankets, a mat
of woven grass, a brazier and a charcoal box, and a table
made from old packing-cases. But there was also a bookshelf made from a wooden box, which held the kind of
books which would normally be found only in a college
library.

It was a strange year which Toyohiko spent in Gamagori. Though he was renewed by long periods of devotional contemplation and the invigoration of an open-air
life, he suffered from the typical depression of tubercular
patients. He learned much from the fishermen and found
them friendly, but they avoided him because of his disease
and provided no intellectual stimulus. To the young man's
astonished pleasure, Myers came and spent four days of his
summer vacation with him, and despite the apparent danger lived and slept with him in the tiny hut. It was an
action which Kagawa never forgot and which, for him,

illustrated the compassion of Christ himself. It was, indeed, another link in the chain which was to draw and finally bind him to his life's work.

Toyohiko was by nature one who eagerly took into his mind and memory every word and experience that came his way. But he was not academic in temper. He was the opposite of the college don who enjoys seclusion and learning for their own sake. Everything was transformed, transmuted, and given out again. In Gamagori, where there was little opportunity for self-expression, he turned to writing. With no money for expensive materials, he used an ordinary writing-brush, black ink and the glossy pages of magazines. His memory ranged over his childhood— the village festivals, the farm and its women-folk, the countryside and the towns of Kobe and Tokushima, his brother Tan-Ichi and his uncle Isobe, who in his imagination became one person, and the struggles he had faced since leaving his uncle's house. All this and much more he poured into a story which was both autobiography and dream. Finally he proudly wrote the title-page, *Like a Dove*, and sent it exultantly to a publisher. Shortly afterwards, cured by a year of hard living, he returned to Kobe to join the ministerial students at the Seminary.

Immediately, he tried to make up for the year that he had lost. Fluent in reading English, he turned to German so that he might read the great theologians and philosophers in their own tongue. He found a professor who owned two sets of the *Japanese Encyclopedia*, and gained one for his own by reading the whole series through from cover to cover. To students and professors alike he was both a puzzling and a promising student, a man of startling promise who drove his own furrow, diverging from the current ecclesiastical attitude which seemed to him to be cruelly and complacently unaware of the real needs of his nation.

31

He was angry and shocked when a bulky parcel arrived from the publishers to whom he had sent his novel. 'Put it in a drawer until you have more experience,' they wrote in a covering letter. It was a lesson in humility which a young man of twenty finds very hard to learn. It seemed to him that no one in the seminary could have had such wide and devastating an experience of life as himself.

On the other hand, he had a genuine kind of Christian humility. It was seen when the case of Professor Aoki, who had given him the encyclopedia, caused a riot amongst the students. The professor, whose teaching methods included chanting the Psalms to the accompaniment of cymbals and drum, was popular both as a teacher and a man. Not unexpectedly, there was jealousy amongst some of his colleagues. Aoki was dismissed. The students refused to attend the classes of the man they believed responsible. Tension grew swiftly and the five ring-leaders of the revolt, including Toyohiko, were expelled at the college assembly. The principal, with cold courtesy, came forward to shake hands after their expulsion. Toyohiko refused to do so. 'I will not make an empty gesture,' he declared. Then he went on to plead the cause of his friends. 'Christianity is a religion of love. A school that teaches love should guide a mistaken student. If God does not abandon us, why should a theological seminary turn us out?' The whole room was still. 'Dismiss me, if you will. I am responsible. But let the others stay.' Myers came down to the college to intervene, and all five were reinstated.

Nevertheless, it had been an uneasy time, and some of the professors shook their heads.

'Young Kagawa is too big for his boots!', said one, bluntly.

'He certainly has a lot to learn. But he has more character than half the others put together.'

'Maybe so. He will find it hard to be a successful minister, though—unless he changes his ways.'

One with more insight broke in: 'I doubt if he *wants* to be what you call a successful minister.'

The objection was obvious: 'But this is a theological seminary. We have opened it for that reason—to train men for the ministry!'

It was Toyohiko himself who solved their dilemma. Working at his studies is not an adequate preparation for the task of a Christian pastor; he must preach, too. Once more, he had joined the pastor who had sent him out before, and gone back to preaching on the borders of Shinkawa. As he did so, his mind cleared. Alongside his objection—almost resentment—to the isolation of the Churches from ordinary life, there had grown up a conviction that God would use him in less orthodox and more dangerous ways. He thought of Canon Barnett's work in the London slums. He recalled the ex-soldier he had seen in Tokushima. He remembered Myers's visit to him in Gamagori. With all these things and the horrors he had witnessed across the river clearly in his mind, he went to talk to his *Sensei*.

'Dr Myers,' he said, quietly, 'I have changed my mind. I do not wish to be ordained. I do not wish to be a minister.'

Myers was taken aback. 'But you have been preparing for it ever since you were turned out of your uncle's home! What do you want to do?'

'I am going to live in the slums.'

On Christmas Day, 1909, Toyohiko Kagawa, a young man of twenty-one, crossed the Higurashi Bridge, the Bridge of the Singing Cicada, to serve his Lord in the slums of Shinkawa.

33

CHAPTER FOUR

Over the Bridge

AN UNWANTED boy once turned to crime because he sought excitement and found, at first, that crime paid well. He developed a technique of his own. Setting fire to a house—an easy business where the houses were made of bamboo and papiermâché—he would wait until the neighbours rushed out to help the unlucky householder. Then, while they were putting the fire out, he would rummage through their houses and be away before they realized they had been robbed. On one occasion, two hundred houses caught fire and the youth was caught. He was jailed, for theft and arson, for nine years. In prison a pickpocket lent him a copy of the Bible, and he came out, at last, determined to lead a new life if someone could show him the way. One day, on the outskirts of Shinkawa, where he made his home, he heard a young man preaching, followed him, asked questions, and was converted.

The ex-convict was Toyohiko's first real contact with the people of the slums. It was he who told the student of a house he could easily rent, since it had been the scene of a murder and was haunted by the dead man's ghost. It was he, too, who pulled the hand-cart across the Higurashi bridge, while Toyohiko pushed behind. There was nothing strange in the little pile of baggage, containing a wicker basket of thin clothes, a roll of bedding and a few cooking-pots, unless it were the books and bamboo book-case thrown alongside them. After stopping to buy some mats for the floor from the grass-mat maker, the two young men pressed on down the alleyway. Even in this cold weather the stench from the open drains was almost unbearable. The cart rattled over the cobbles and their wooden clogs slithered over the wet filth underfoot. On each side, where the low, smelly huts were joined one to another, unkempt women stood in the doorways, while the men, watching with suspicious eyes, scarcely bothered to edge out of the way. Only when they stopped by the empty hut did the ragged children, with their dirt-streaked faces, stop following and calling after them. The new man was going to live in the haunted house. The people of the alley glanced at each other and shrugged their shoulders. He could not be right in the head.

Toyohiko looked at the hut and felt sick. It was six feet by nine, like every other one in the lane. Its walls were made of bamboo, but there was no paper in the windows or in the flimsy entrance door. The floors were fouled by dogs, and vermin crawled everywhere. Toyohiko held his heaving stomach, prayed for courage and went inside, where a thin partition divided the hut into two tiny rooms. Borrowing a broom, he began to clean up. Darkness, falling quickly, had almost come before he had finished. The ex-convict went away, and Toyohiko, because he had had no money to buy oil for his lamp, sat cross-legged on the floor, listening, thinking and praying.

Outside, the unceasing noise of the slums went on—a shrill chatter of sound, broken by children's cries, the sharp outbreaks of quarrels and slurred voices of drunken men and women. The smell of the slums had already begun to cling to his clothes and his body. Alone except for a diseased dog which had slunk inside the hut, he wondered if he were mad to have done this thing which no one could understand. On the other side of the bridge it had seemed the only step to take. If these people were to be won for Christ, he must come and live amongst them. Now he wondered if he could even spend a whole night here. His mind ranged backwards to the quiet beauty of Awa, to the ceremonious tea-drinking of his uncle's house and the peace of the college library. His breath dragged up from his weak lungs, painfully and slowly. Still praying, he fell asleep.

Sleep did not seem to last long. The slum-dwellers were about before dawn, and Toyohiko took his place in the queue waiting at the stand-pipe for water. They looked at him incredulously, astonished that this frail young man should have some power which had held the ghost of the house at bay. They said little, apart from asking his name. His presence turned them suddenly silent.

Each of the great cities of Japan had its slum-area, and Kobe's Shinkawa was typical of the worst of them. In eleven main alleyways, with narrow lanes crossing at right-angles, lived eleven thousand people. Some were dockers, factory-workers, street-cleaners, the underpaid servants of the community who could not afford to live anywhere else, but to Shinkawa, too, came the unwanted—the mentally ill, the beggars, the chronically sick. In its labyrinthine alleys the criminals sought refuge, knowing that the police would not trouble to root them out. Murderers, pick-pockets, gamblers, epileptics, prostitutes, drunkards, rag-pickers—Toyohiko saw them all that morning as he watched. In addition, there were the children. Boys, girls and babies ran and crawled everywhere.

The revulsion of the previous night was still in his stomach, but a new light shone in his eyes. He had done the right thing, and with God's help he would stay. These people needed education and schools, medical care and clinics, moral welfare and food-centres. More than all, they needed Christ. He must preach to them. But, to do that, he must live with them.

The Protestant Church had come to Japan scarcely half a century earlier. It had hardly begun to establish itself in the towns, much less the country. It had not even begun to touch the slums where there seemed to be no religion of any kind at all. Toyohiko saw that the poor would never accept something which was offered to them by the wealthy or respectable folk who came from across the river, dispensed their charitable gospel, and then went back home. The Church must be planted here in the slums, tended day and night. Only then would it grow.

Because they knew nothing of the compulsion which had driven him to Shinkawa, the slum-dwellers could not understand what he was or wanted to do. If he had not run away from home and was not a criminal, they decided, then he must be a police spy. When they found that this was not so either, they did not know what to make of him. Their bewilderment, however, did not prevent some of them from trying to sponge on him. It was their nature to get what they could from an unwary stranger, even if it was only free food and lodging.

'*Gomen nasai*,' said a whining voice outside the hut on the first evening. 'Please excuse me!'

Toyohiko came out and saw a loathsome-looking young man staring at him, his face and body dreadful with dermatitis.

'What can I do for you?'

It was a strange greeting. Most people drove him away as soon as they saw him. 'There is room for more than one in that big hut.' Toyohiko nodded agreement. 'Can I share it with you?'

The student—he was still to attend classes at the seminary for a while—remembered how his friends had driven the beggar out of his room in Tokyo. There was no one now to save him from himself, but he did not want to share his room. Already he realized that one of the most dreadful things about the slum was its lack of privacy. Yet he could not preach about love without demonstrating it. He stood aside and, with a courteous gesture, beckoned the man to enter.

The next night another man came. He had once been a bean-curd vendor, but a drunkard had knocked his stall over in the early morning, spilling the food all over the street. Angrily he had knocked the drunken man over in his turn, and there, amongst the spilled curds, he had died. The curd-seller had been sent to prison for murder. Now that he was out again the ghost of his victim haunted him and would not leave him alone. That night he went to sleep peacefully on Toyohiko's mat, while the young man held his hand.

The third night it was an alcoholic, a purple-faced man who spent the time he was not drinking leaning against the bamboo wall of some hut or other. One after the other, for a night, or a few nights, or hoping to stay indefinitely, the vagrants moved in. Toyohiko's peace was gone for ever.

Not surprisingly, when the notions of being a criminal or a police-spy had been dispelled, another rumour gained ground. He was slightly mad; he must be the only son of a rich landowner, who was following the Buddhist way of salvation, and was trying to reach Nirvana by giving away everything he possessed. If that were so, why should not the poor help him to achieve his end? It was not entirely a cynical attitude. Even in the industrialized society of the new Japan, Buddhism, with its doctrine of merit and good works, had a firm hold. Almsgiving was a normal feature of life. The poor and the beggars expected nothing more.

The rich, who dispensed charity after the traditional manner, had no need to think of improving standards of life for the poor, so long as they gave them a coin or so.

How far all this was from the truth, few people at first guessed. Toyohiko did not talk about money. He could manage with next to nothing for himself. That, indeed, was all he had. A scholarship from the college gave him ten *yen* a month. A job sweeping chimneys brought him another eleven *yen*. Altogether it amounted to about ten shillings a week. Even amongst the poor, it was not enough to provide much for four men. Rice-gruel, thinned down with water, was all Toyohiko could afford to offer his guests. He himself always had less than the other three, but that was something they never seemed to notice.

The first weeks and months in Shinkawa followed a fairly regular pattern. Toyohiko rose before dawn, spent some time in meditation—a Buddhist habit which had long ago become part of his Christian practice—and went out to wash and collect water at the hydrant which served the twenty families at his end of the lane. At six o'clock in the morning he stood and preached to all who would listen at one of the crossings. The morning he spent working at college or sweeping chimneys. Some days at two o'clock he would preach again; on others, he spoke in the evening. In between, he talked to all who would listen, or read and wrote in his hut, despite the men and women who seemed to make it their own at all hours of the day and night. The children became his friends long before their parents had accepted him, and he could always be recognized in the alleyways by the crowd of dirty urchins who followed him round. Slowly, as the weeks went by, he was accepted. The idea that he had unlimited money lost ground. He became known as 'the preacher' and, a little later, as 'the Christian'—one of the very few in

Shinkawa. Not unnaturally, alongside those who listened and wanted to hear more, there were others who imposed on him, or disliked and scorned him. Not a few tried to drive him away by violence.

When a drunken man tried to stab him as he began preaching, Toyohiko took to his heels while the crowd jeered at him for a coward. But he was back next day in the same place, preaching once more.

A bully knocked him over, breaking four of his teeth. A gambler burst into his hut, kicked the brazier over, and left him to beat out the fire with his bare hands. Others smashed the flimsy door of his hut, stole his clothing and broke his furniture. An angry brothel-owner threatened him with a pistol because he preached against prostitution.

None of them knew much about him. None knew anything about Christianity. All of them recognized the power of his pacifism and his refusal to hit back, and saw in his presence a force which would destroy the evil by which they lived.

In the same way, he was the victim of lazy and persuasive beggars. To one he gave food, to another clothes. To one who demanded his coat, he gave his shirt and trousers, being reduced to wearing a red *kimono* thrown into the hut by a kindly woman neighbour. He seemed to be without resentment. 'Love', as he preached and practised it, was an unknown word in the vocabulary of either criminals or Buddhists, but as the weeks went by, it took on a meaning clothed with the flesh of Toyohiko himself. He longed that those who knew and heard him would come to know the love of the incarnate Christ. That they might do so, he would give all he had.

'Penniless and without food I can live. Penniless I can share my rags. But I cannot bear to hear hungry children cry.' So he wrote—to his neighbours he seemed always to be writing—in one of his note-books. He had become used to the noise of the slums. Quarrels raged in the houses round him every day. He counted seven murders in his own alleyway in the first year he spent there. Prostitution and drunkenness, gambling and cruelty were everywhere about him. He hated it all and longed to change it, but two things, in those first months, nearly broke his heart— the indifference of those about him to God, and the indifference of the folk across the river to people of Shinkawa.

> *I came to bring*
> *God to the slum;*
> *But I am dumb,*
> > *Dismayed;*
> > *Betrayed*
> > *By those*
> *Whom I would aid;*
> > *Pressed down,*
> > *So sad*
> > *I fear*
> > *That I am mad.*
>
> > *Pictures*
> *Race through my brain*
> > *And lie*
> > *Upon my heart.*
> *Pictures like this:*
> > *A man*
> *Legs rotted off*
> *With syphilis;*
> > *And yet,*
> *He need not fret*
> *That money*
> *Does not come,*
> *Because his wife*

Is rented out
And brings
Sufficient sum.
One month in the slums,
And I am sad,
So sad
I seem devil-possessed,
Or mad.

. . . here are the slippery streets, which are never dry;
They are lined with open sewers, where rats come out to die;
Tattered paper doors stand wide to winds that beat;
The houses are all of a reddish black, like the hue of stale whale meat;
Filth on the flimsy ceilings, dirt in the musty air;
Elbowed out of their crowded rooms, people are everywhere;
All night long they crouch in the cold, huddled on broken benches,
Where there's never a moment's lifting of the heavy offal stenches.

The painted idiot-girl,
Upon whose back
Vile pictures
Were tattooed
In red,
Will never lure men to her den again;
She is dead. . . .

You ordinary folk
Upon the hill,
To whom
The slums are vague,
Listen and tremble
As I scream to you,
'SHE DIED OF PLAGUE!'
I hear
A harsh voice
Cry out,

'Here you! Dance!'
I see a thin child dodge
And I know
It is the boy
Whose father
       Kicks him.
Twelve years old,
Driven from bed
Into the streets,
Naked and cold. . . .

I must be done with thoughts like these!
The raindrops patter from the eaves;
The fire beneath my half-boiled rice is out;
I hear the rising roar of ribald shout
That brings the evening to Shinkawa Slum.

IS THERE NO WAY
THAT HELP CAN COME?

CHAPTER FIVE

The Love-story of Miss Spring

IT WAS impossible to win the slum-dwellers of Shinkawa for Christ merely by living amongst them and preaching to them. Precept and example were of urgent importance—there was no doubt about that; but much more must be done if the love of Christ were to spread through this grim under-world. Toyohiko's youthful idealism began to give place to a more realistic assessment of the situation.

'Kagawa *San*!' The respectful greeting, as he passed by the bamboo houses, always busy but never in too much of a hurry to stop, was often the prelude to an earnest request or an awkward confession. As the months went by, he became the trusted confidant of scores of unhappy people. Women talked to him about their husbands, fathers about their children, young people about their work. Few of them wanted to know more about the Gospel he preached, but in his eager compassion for their needs he seldom failed to commend the Lord he loved. Again and again, his sincere interest in the affairs of his neighbours provided an opening for a heart-to-heart talk about God. Probably, to most of Shinkawa's populace he was a queer figure, but he was a figure of some consequence. Respect was touched by confidence in his judgement and affection for his deep humanity.

There were those whom he could never influence. Drink-sodden men who had lost the power to think or love, drug-addicts who would commit murder for money to buy new supplies, baby-farmers who were paid to take away unwanted children and then slowly starved them to death, vice-racketeers who had long ago lost any moral scruples they might once have possessed—to such as these he was an enemy to be avoided or pursued. But it must not be imagined that Shinkawa, or the slums of any of the big cities, were made up entirely of criminals, imbeciles and outcasts from society.

Japan, in the early days of the twentieth century, despite its growing industrial and commercial wealth, was a poor country. Riches were concentrated in the hands of the few. Peasants, fishermen, labourers and common workmen were deplorably underpaid. When they were too ill or too old to work they were dismissed without any thought for their welfare. The laws, framed to protect the wealthy classes who made them, prohibited any sort of trade union or even any united action amongst the workers to demand better conditions. Inevitably, the old, the sick, the infirm and thousands of the workers themselves found cheap homes in Shinkawa's bamboo houses. There was nowhere else for them to go. Not unnaturally, many fell into the vicious habits of their neighbours.

'I cling to men. I love them. I can't help loving them!' So Kagawa wrote in his *Meditations*. The most colourful stories from his early period in the slums concern his encounters with gamblers, bullies and drunkards who tried to murder him. His love was big enough to forgive such creatures, many of them far gone beyond his power to save them. But in general his service was given to the aged, the children, the workers, the decent folk who made some response to it. It was on them, and with their help, that the next stage of his work was founded.

Some little time after he moved in, the house two doors away fell vacant. Toyohiko rented it at once. A scheme for consolidating his haphazard work of preaching and charity was beginning to form in his mind. People seldom stayed long in one place, and shortly afterwards the two houses in between became available. Toyohiko took down the slim dividing walls between the houses and threw them into a long, narrow hall. Temporary screens and partitions were easy to erect when necessary, either by day or night. He was ready to begin some kind of organized work.

Homeless people always saddened him. He already had the haunted murderer, the alcoholic and others. Now he made room for an old pipe-mender, Kishimoto, bent double with rheumatism, and his wife, whose father had been retainer to one of the old feudal lords in the mountain country. A teen-age delinquent, Matsuzo, joined them. Matsuzo, in his turn, came across a twisted beggar-woman living in a hen-coop on a rubbish-dump and brought her to the 'hall'. The extended bamboo house might well have been called a hostel, except that no one paid any rent, and few contributed to the cost of their food. They repaid Toyohiko in other ways. The young criminal, Matsuzo, began to change into an eager young student. Kishimoto and his wife cleaned the house, fetched water and did some of the cooking. When a widow with five young children asked for shelter there was little she could contribute, but she turned the strange little community into a family.

Just about this time, Toyohiko heard that his stepmother, Michi, had finally had to leave the tumble-down quarters she lived in at Awa. In the years that followed his departure from his island home at Shikoku he had kept in touch with Awa, and even his dismissal by Uncle Isobe had not broken the relationship with Michi. Family ties are strong in Japan, and Toyohiko knew that his grandmother had died and his sister Ei was married. His two younger brothers were making their way in the world, one apprenticed to a rich merchant and the other to a small industrial concern. Neither of them could do much to help Michi. Indeed, unlike Toyohiko, they scarcely knew her, for they had not lived at Awa but had been adopted by relatives after Denjiro Kagawa's death. If anyone were to help it must be Toyohiko. He rented a tiny house on the outskirts of Shinkawa and established his stepmother there, where he could visit her each day. Her disgust at the conditions under which Toyohiko lived, when he could by this time have been in some distinguished if junior government post, gave way to a new respect and affection for him. She knew what it meant to be poor and live on the charity of others. After a while she began to brave the horrors of the slums to come and help her stepson in his busy life.

The 'hall', of course, was no mere home for the homeless. Toyohiko needed a centre for his evangelistic work. Every Sunday, and on other evenings of the week, he used it as a preaching-centre. His Sunday-school was held there, too, until it became so big that, except when it rained, he had to run it out of doors in an unused open space. In time he was able to establish a small dispensary, with the occasional clinical services of a doctor.

All this made heavy demands on money, time and health. Toyohiko was still not completely recovered from the tuberculosis that had driven him to the fishing-village on Atzuma Bay. More than once he collapsed when preaching in the open-air and had to be carried home. In addition, he contracted a disease which was to worry him even more than his lung-trouble. The beggar whom he had taken in on his first arrival in Shinkawa suffered from trachoma, a painful eye-disease that may cause partial or complete blindness, and Toyohiko became infected with it. It greatly distressed him and made writing or reading impossible for long periods; later it robbed him of the sight of one eye.

Help came from the college and the churches as Toyo-hiko's work extended. Missionary wives and Japanese Christians came down to assist with the Sunday-school, and later with distributing food to the beggars. Money was harder to find than helpers. There were grants from the College and occasional gifts from Christian friends. It seemed like a fortune when an unknown American, who had heard from Myers of Toyohiko's work, promised to send fifty dollars a month. With it, plans were made for more extension. Always, however, there seemed more bills to pay than there was money to meet them. Toyohiko remembered the novel he had written with such high hopes at Gamagori, and began to write.

It was not easy. Some writing could be done in the mornings, when the hut was comparatively empty. But much of it had to be done at night, by the light of an oil lamp, when the occupants of the house were asleep. There were many mornings when, as the dawn began to filter through the narrow interstices of the bamboo walls, Kishi-moto and his wife roused from their blankets to see Toyo-hiko sitting cross-legged in the middle of the floor, still writing, unaware that the night had gone and he had not slept.

His first book, written the year after he came to Shin-kawa, was for children. Entitled *Friendship*, it was the story of David and Jonathan. The following year, 1911, he published *Jeremiah the Prophet*. Two years later, there came *The History of the Agitation Concerning the Life of Christ*. At the same time, he was working on studies of *The Psychology of Fear* and *The Psychology of Poverty*. Meanwhile, too, something else was happening which was to mean more to him than any success he might achieve with his books. Toyo-hiko, to his great surprise, was falling in love.

One of his tasks was to help a Christian pastor from Kobe who took services in a bookbinding factory. From time to time, when the pastor had other duties, Toyohiko would visit the factory, with its forty or so women workers, and try to interest them in the Christian faith. The owner was himself a Christian, who insisted that his workpeople should come to the services. Most of them were dull, uninterested and sleepy in this midday break. It did not take Toyohiko long to see that one of the few who really listened was a forewoman, a girl of somewhere about his own age. He was thankful for her interest, but thought no more of it.

Haruko Shiba was, in fact, almost Toyohiko's age—indeed, according to Japanese custom, where age was always reckoned from New Year's Day, she was exactly the same. She had been born at Yokusuka, near Yokohama, but her prosperous family had fallen on bad times while she was still a child and had moved to Osaka. She had hoped to be a teacher. Instead, she had had to find work as housemaid and had then moved on to the bookbindery, where she had been put in charge of a department of forty girls. Her wages had risen to sixpence a day. During the years that followed, she saw and thought a good deal of Toyohiko, from a distance. He had helped the Kobe pastor at the factory from the time he was a student at the seminary. After his immersion in the work of the mission-hall in Shinkawa, however, he gave less time to it. If Haru asked about him, she heard only that he was preaching in the slums. Then, one day, she came across a little straggling group on the outskirts of Shinkawa. The listeners were poor apprentices, diseased prostitutes, labourers and beggars. The singers appeared to be factory workers and old people. Haru had almost passed by when a new figure joined the group—young, thin, dressed in a striped kimono with a black sash, and wearing wooden clogs which clattered on the cobbles. If his face were filled out a little he would be handsome, she was thinking. Then, suddenly, she recognized him and stood still, her interest gripped. It was not only Haru who was held when Toyohiko arrived; the singers gained new energy, and the slouching listeners straightened and moved forward. There seemed a magnetism about him even before he started to speak, and when he began his voice held an authority that immediately swelled the crowd. Even in those early days his power to move his listeners was evident.

Life began to change for Haru Shiba. Her first name means 'Spring'. It was as though her personality had started to match her name. Her thinking developed; her dreams were full of hope. The dull days which had been filled with the smell of paper and glue, and the pleasant nights spent in her favourite recreation, the theatre, burgeoned into new life. She made her way to the mission hall with her sister Fuji as chaperone, and though she stood outside not daring to go in, Toyohiko saw her. He came to talk to her at the factory and persuaded her to come regularly. But he began to feel uneasy.

Leave me alone, love;
Leave my heart alone.

Toyohiko began to realize that she did not come merely because she wanted to hear what he had to say; she came because she wanted to see him. In his heart a strange conflict began to make itself felt. At his age most men were marrying, if indeed they had not already a wife and a family. Marriage had had no place in his own plans. There was too much for him to do. There were too many needy people to love. Now, he longed for someone to share his work. His brush-pen drooped in his hand as he sat cross-legged under the light of the lamp, trying to put some order into his thoughts about the psychology of poverty. His thoughts turned to spring, to the melting snow on Mount Fuji, to the almond blossom at Awa, to Haru, 'Miss Spring' herself. When he wrote, it was not about the psychology of poverty, but about the conflict of vocation and love.

> *Love, linger not to whisper your temptation,*
> *Seek not to bind me with your heavy chain.*
> *I would be free to seek the world's salvation,*
> *I would be free to rescue men from pain.*

The conflict only began to be resolved when Haru told him that her parents had found her a suitable husband. Toyohiko, like a dutiful Japanese, counselled filial obedience—and in his heart hoped she would do what few women in Japan would dare to do. He hardly knew what to say when Haru told him she would never marry a non-Christian, and added that she would prefer to work in the slums with him. In a land where not even men proposed marriage directly but only through the family elders, and women would not dream of speaking of it in such a way, it was a bizarre conversation, almost unthinkable. Haru hurriedly repented of her boldness and went away. Toyohiko wrote a letter, making a direct proposal of marriage, and Haru, who had defied so many conventions, replied stiffly that this was not the way matters should be arranged. Toyohiko followed her, and one day, when the spring was bursting into life on every side, found her on the beach, apologized for his way of doing things, and then, forgetting his apology, asked her once more to marry him.

For Japan, it was a strange courtship. For Haru, it was the prelude to a period of unending work and grim poverty. For Toyohiko, it was the end of solitariness. They were married in the Kobe church by Dr Harry Myers in May

1914, six months after Haru's baptism in Toyohiko's mission hut. The wedding was as lovely as music, flowers and friends could make it. To complete the day's joy, it should have been followed by a honeymoon under the delicate blossoms of a Japanese springtime, within sight of the blue sea. Instead, bride and bridegroom clambered into a jinriksha and gave their order to the pulling-boy: 'Shinkawa!'

Weddings in the East as well as the West have their practical jokers, and at first the boy refused to believe them. He was still shaking his head in bewilderment when he helped them down outside the mission hut, amongst a growing crowd of excited, shrill children and workpeople. Haru's first night of marriage was spent in a hut shared by the unwanted, and the first meal she cooked next morning was for fourteen besides themselves. But despite the crowds and the dirt, life was sweet. There was little money to spare and much to do with it, but there was sunshine. They had the hut, and each other.

> *Bright sunshine*
> *On a hut—*
> *Our little hut—*
> *Where we stand,*
> *My love and I,*
> *Heart to heart,*
> *Hand in hand.*
>
> *As the springtime buds*
> *Grow, close together,*
> *So shall we grow,*
> *For ever and for ever.*

It was Haru who insisted that, if she were going to be of any real service to her husband, she must to some extent match him in education. Toyohiko agreed. It was not a case of beginning from the beginning. Japan had for long tried to ensure a minimum standard of literacy, and Haru would not have held her position in the bindery if she had not had a basic education. Now, however, she rose each morning to join a little group of working men who clustered round Toyohiko before they went to work, learning algebra and geometry. Later on, she went each morning to the Women's Bible School in Kobe to learn more about the Scriptures. When the Bible School was closed, she studied with her husband in the high-school classes he ran either in the morning or between five and six o'clock in the evening.

Life was hard. Study, cleaning and cooking would have been sufficiently demanding if their home had been an ordinary one in a Kobe suburb. Instead, they had to live on an income of £3 a month, for the monthly fifty dollars from America had ceased, in a crowded hut that was preaching-place and hostel, taking their turn at a water-hydrant and a toilet which each served a hundred people. Haru watched as her husband wrote down his deepest thoughts, with tears in his eyes.

> *You who dwell*
> *In the heart of my heart,*
> *Listen to me;*
>
> *This you must know—*
> *I am a child of grief and pain,*
> *Bending my fingers to count my woe.*
>
> *You yield me*
> *Everything;*
> *But I*
> *Have nothing*
> *I can bring*
> *To give to you.*

Know
You have married
Poverty, sorrow;
Bear it with me;
The storm will be over
Tomorrow.

A little while
For us
The rod;
And then,
Then, God!

Haru had married not only poverty and sorrow. She had married, though she did not realize it at the beginning, a man who would always be wandering, and not infrequently to the earth's end.

The first of his journeys he took a few months after they were married. Toyohiko decided that, if he were to serve men as he ought, he must see something other than Japan. He must go and study in America. There was no money, of course, to pay the fare; but Michi, his stepmother, gave him a little from her savings and so did one of his younger brothers. Dr Myers and Dr Logan sought help from the Church in Kobe and from the seminary. Arrangements were made for Haru to attend a concentrated study-course while he was away, and three days after war broke out in Europe, in August 1914, Toyohiko set sail for the United States.

He had enrolled at Princeton University, but because of his wide book-knowledge was excused classes as long as he submitted a thesis. Instead of class-room work, he investigated the social services and the living conditions of American slums. For eighteen months he toured through the big cities, moving from west to east and back again.

He gained his doctorate in philosophy without difficulty, but it was his least important acquisition.

'The slums are a laboratory of life and of human society,' he wrote. 'I am doing research work with the slum as my laboratory and man as my special subject.' It was a work he had begun in Shinkawa and intended to continue. But his two years in America gave him a new attitude to it. Without losing his love of human beings he gained a new interest in sociology and economics. Infant mortality was high where wages were low. Tuberculosis was rife where men were under-nourished and hours of work too long. Prostitution was the consequence of poverty. Drink was an escape-mechanism. Labour demanded legislation. He had known these things, but they were clarified in the American setting. He had been so busy working amongst the slum-people that he had not thought about dealing with the problem of the slums themselves.

He returned at last to Shinkawa, to Haru and the mission-hut. But he was a different man. He had left the slums a social worker. He returned a reformer.

CHAPTER SIX

'Across the Death-line'

THINGS HAD changed while Toyohiko was away from Kobe. They had changed in his own family. Michi, his stepmother, cared for with true Japanese filial piety and Christian love, had died. Haru, free of the hut in the slums and working in the Bible School, had achieved all she had longed for as a girl, and graduated alongside students much junior to her. Things had changed in Japan itself, for the country, involved in the war on the British and American side, was extending its industry and drawing more and more workers into the factories, docks and shipyards.

Back in Shinkawa, where he immediately returned with his wife, Toyohiko found that the slums themselves were unaltered. On the other hand, to his deep distress, he soon saw that some of the things for which he had laboured so hard were already lost. The mission-hut was still there, and services were continuing, led by his friends and supporters from the town churches and the mission—but something had happened to the people. Without his personal interference on the side of righteousness the young people had failed to withstand the forces of evil. Three of the girls had been sold as prostitutes, and forty of the boys were in prison for theft and other crimes.

But if there were changes in the land and people, Toyohiko Kagawa himself had changed too. He was still comparatively young, not quite thirty, but his knowledge was

greater, his judgement more shrewd and his horizons greatly
widened. Up to the time he left for America, he had been
content to preach a gospel of love and practise it in helping
individuals. Now, he was aware that the problem of poverty
itself would have to be tackled.

His quiet voice growing shrill with eagerness, he talked
incessantly to his wife and his Japanese and American
friends about what he had seen and what he longed to do.
His tumbling sentences were interpreted and his points
emphasized by sweeping gestures and stabbing movements
of his thin hands.

'There are two and a half million people on the Japanese
labour-roll. Did you know that?' He never paused for an
answer in those long dissertations. 'They're in transport,
docks, factories, mines and the Public Works Department.
They're underpaid and overworked.'

'Well?'

'If they were in Britain or America they could stand up
for themselves, organize themselves to fight for their own
rights. Here in our country they would be imprisoned if
they attempted anything of the kind. You may sell your
daughter to a brothel and no one takes any notice; try to
form a Trades Union and you will be punished more
harshly than if you knock an old woman down and rob her.'

'But what can we do to stop it?' His friends seemed
always to make the same answer without seeing the obvious
solution. 'It happens because men are too poor to support
their families.'

Kagawa's finger stabbed the air again. 'Exactly. We
must get rid of poverty . . . force the Government to
acknowledge the workers' right to form unions . . . sweep
away the slums.'

'*We?*' The reply was sharp. 'Who do you mean by "we?"'

'The Church. Christian people who care. You pastors

E   57

and your congregations outside the slums. My wife and myself.'

At first he was astonished at the glances which his listeners exchanged with each other. There was embarrassment, anger and hostility in them. 'No, Kagawa *San*. Live in the slums if that's your way. Try and lift people up by preaching the gospel. But don't involve yourself in politics. It's a dirty business and it's dangerous. It will bring the Church into disrepute. You know we're only a small group, we Christians. It wouldn't be difficult for the Government to restrict our work. You mustn't risk it.'

The young reformer sighed, lifting his hands and then dropping them helplessly. Talk about political action or economic schemes and the reply was always the same. 'It isn't the job of the Church.'

Kagawa saw that his future was bound up with three demands. He must show that Christianity was not a pietistic way of life, remote from the joyful and dirty business of living; it involved the Church's sharing in life as much as her Master had done. This must be demonstrated by his continuing to live in the limiting, sordid environment of Shinkawa. But alongside his practical compassion, he must go out in the name of Christ and try to find some solution to the labour problem of Japan. It was already clear that, in doing this, he would alienate many of his fellow-Christians as well as expose himself to Government wrath.

Partly to make plain his close association with the Church, and partly because he felt God called him to fulfil the vow he had postponed, Kagawa was ordained into the Christian Ministry in 1917. One of the ministers who shared in the service had been amongst his attackers a dozen years earlier at the High School in Tokyo. The fact was illustrative of the way in which critics joined the ranks of his supporters as the years passed. Refusing to take over the pastorate of a city church, he continued to exercise his ministry in Shinkawa.

Some little time previously, in Tokyo, an enthusiastic friend of the workers, Bunji Suzuki, had organized the *Yuai Kai*, the 'Labourers' Benefit Society'. A kind of co-operative organization, it could hardly be outlawed by the Government. Now Suzuki was going farther, and beginning a Japanese Federation of Labour. The trouble was that so few labourers had the ability to deal with such administrative work, and no one but labourers and a few high-minded citizens were likely to assist the project. Least of all would help have been sought in the respectable ranks of the Church. In Kobe, however, it was from the Church that the most effective leadership emerged. Toyohiko Kagawa, the Christian minister, to the horror of not a few fellow-workers, became the founder of the Kobe branch and began to build up its membership amongst the labourers on the docks. Soon afterwards he became the National Secretary of the Federation. He was nominated as the Japanese representative to the International Labour Office, but turned down the honour to deal with matters closer at hand.

Officialdom watched him and did not like what it saw. It was already clear to the magistrates and police of Kobe that, if the growing mood of insurgence amongst the dock-workers burst into open trouble, the young Christian minister would be somewhere in the middle of it. He was far from being a national figure, except in Christian circles, but in Kobe his name was becoming familiar. One afternoon a reporter set out to exploit this new interest.

Wandering through Shinkawa, protecting his Western clothes from the filth in the lanes and the wet washing hanging across the alleys, the journalist found his way to Kagawa's hut. The preacher was out and so was his wife.

One or two old people, lying in the preaching-room which was also a hostel, greeted him without much interest. Strangers were always seeking Kagawa *San* these days. They waved him into the Kagawa's private room—a privacy guaranteed, as the journalist soon saw, only by a flimsy door and papered bamboo walls. Though it lacked many things, the room had character. It was clean and uncrowded. On a bookshelf made from a wooden crate stood piles of books. Their titles were astonishing, and in some cases unreadable to the visitor, for they were the classic volumes in Japanese, English and German, on modern economics and sociology.

On top of the bookshelf stood a pile of manuscript. The journalist took it up casually, flicked over the pages, and began to read. Astonishment deepened on his solemn face. Here was something better than material for an article on a politically-minded Christian minister. Here, surely, was the man himself, burning through the long pages of a novel.

In his hut, as the noises of the streets died away, Kagawa had taken out the book he had written in the fishing-village of Gamagori. He knew now what the publisher had meant when he had talked about 'more experience of life'. Sitting cross-legged, or kneeling by the low table in the centre of the tiny hut, he had re-written the story of Eiichi, the bombastic young idealist. Home, college, tea-house, municipal office, lodging-house, the country and the slums were the background of the story he had told. It was a relief and a release from the growing demands of the labourers. When at last it was finished, he had laid it on the top of his book-shelves.

'A man came to see you,' said one of the 'lodgers' in the big hut when Kagawa returned. 'He came from a news-paper.'

'He took something away,' added another, not bothering to get up. 'And he said he had left a letter for you.'

The letter lay where the manuscript had been. Kagawa opened it and stood for a long time, holding it in trembling hands after he had read it. There was a receipt for the manuscript and a promise on behalf of the editor to pay him twelve hundred and fifty *yen*—two hundred and fifty pounds—for the first serial rights. He could not believe his own eyes, and set off to interview the newspaper-man. But it was quite true. The novel from which he had hoped so much was translated into English and serialized in the *Japan Chronicle* of Kobe, the leading English language newspaper in the country, edited by Robert Young.

As a serial it raised some interest without causing any great stir. A year or two later it would do much more. But, from Kagawa's point of view, its immediate results were of tremendous value. It provided funds to help in work amongst labourers. It made it possible to open a free clinic in Shinkawa, in 1918, with a nurse in attendance, and to begin a night-school for labourers in Osaka. The following year the Shinkawa clinic was extended, and a full-time doctor was employed.

No one really quite knew what to make of Kagawa. He was a phenomenon without parallel in Japan, though part of the inspiration for the ministry he exercised had come from men who acted in much the same way in other countries. He fitted into no pattern. He was a minister without a church, a doctor in philosophy with qualifications for teaching in a university who chose to run high-school classes for common labourers, a Christian who was openly critical of respectable Japanese Christianity, a pacifist who was prepared to stir up trouble. The hostility of the Church mounted, and continued to do so for many years. Christian leaders sincerely believed he was wrong to involve the Church in politics when its real task was saving souls. The result was that Kagawa's own profound and mystical faith has not always been recognized, simply because he himself had to stand so firmly by his belief that, in William Temple's phrase, Christianity was the most materialistic of all religions. In fact, few Christians of his day—and perhaps none in the East—so faithfully united in their religious philosophy the mystical and practical elements of the faith.

To the officials of Kobe, who knew little about Christianity except that the Church was suspicious of the young man in the slums, the problem was clear. Toyohiko Kagawa was merely another agitator, active at a time when Trades Unionists and Communists were becoming too common, and he would have to be restrained. The chance to restrain him appeared to be given them by Kagawa himself.

In 1919 he published a book called *The Adoration of the Labourer*. It was just what Kobe officialdom had waited for. Even the title was an offence. Kagawa was arrested, taken to court and charged with seditious intentions. The court found him awkward, not because he ranted at them as they hoped and expected, but because he refused to be put out of temper. For the first time the magistrates faced a Christian pacifist who really believed that even law-courts and magistrates could be won over by love. The court records indicate the way he behaved: 'He *appears* moderate, temperate and sound.'

What the officials actually thought lies in the next sentence. 'He is really crafty, sly, subtle, insidious, designing, treacherous and double-faced; and though advancing radical theories gives the impression of cherishing revolutionary ideas.' They would have imprisoned him if they had been able, but in fact there was nothing for which they could hold him, and they had to let him go. He went home, to what he described as his 'six-foot shack in the slums'. He hated it more than ever, not for himself but because of all it symbolized of the degradation around him.

> *I can see*
>> *No hope*
> *For the slums*
> *Because that*
> *First of all*
>> *This thing*
>> *Is wrong—*
>> *That men*
> *Should crowd*
> *Thus in the dearth,*
>> *And dark,*
>> *And dirt—*
> *Should crowd and throng . . .*

His mind was beating about the problem of poverty more urgently. For him it had, at that moment, two special aspects. Both must be dealt with. The first was the problem of the slums themselves. While they existed they would always be a cess-pit from which vice, crime and evil would crawl to pollute the country. They ought to be swept away. Reformers were beginning to agree about this, but the generality of the population were as untouched by their existence as those to whom he had addressed his first violent poem in *Songs From the Slums*. How could people be made aware of this running sore on the fair body of Japan? The second problem was that, even if the slums were somehow swept out of existence, so long as labourers were not paid a living wage and were forbidden to negotiate or strike under penalty of imprisonment, they would inevitably recreate the slums all over again.

These two problems were focused sharply in the public

eye, and set on the way to solution, in 1920 and 1921.

A publisher had read the serialized version of Kagawa's novel in the *Japan Chronicle*, and feeling it deserved a wider public, he approached the author. 'Will you re-edit it and lengthen it?' he asked. 'Make it about half as long again as its present size. Concentrate in the new part on the slums.' Kagawa did so, working feverishly in the intervals of superintending the clinics, teaching at night-schools in Osaka and Kobe, preaching in his mission-hall and out of doors, and attending to the growing demands of the Federation of Labour. He brought Eiichi, his hero, into the slums, and the miseries and Christian courage of his characters matched those he himself had known. The publisher believed he had a novel of genius, and advertised it as such. Japan is a highly literate country, and books were widely bought. The name of Toyohiko Kagawa was becoming known as a labour leader. But none of this prepared either author or publisher for the success that came to them.

Across the Death-line, published in 1920, created a phenomenal stir hardly ever known before in Japanese publishing history. Its first edition was sold out immediately, and printing after printing was required to meet the public demand. As an author, Kagawa's fame was nation-wide. For some time it sold at the rate of a hundred thousand copies a year. To him it was more important that the attention of the whole country was turned to the existence of the slums.

The following year his name leaped into the headlines once more. This time, however, it was notoriety rather than fame that he achieved.

Towards the middle of 1921, thirty thousand labourers in the Mitsubishi and Kawasaki dockyards of Kobe determined to go on strike. Knowing that Kagawa was in sympathy with them, they surged down the Shinkawa alleys and out to the Labour Federation's office in Kobe, carrying banners, spades, picks, and yelling at the tops of their shrill voices.

'Lead us, Kagawa! Lead us, Kagawa!' Banners and shouts carried the same message.

Addressing the swollen crowd of angry men, Kagawa promised to lead them if they would refrain from violence. They must unite—and they must not go back to work. The news was sent out all over the country. Kagawa, the famous pacifist-author from the slums, had called the dock-labourers out on strike and formed a Trades Union. He had defied the Government and broken the law. But in spite of his illegal activities, the police had to admit that the strikers were remarkably peaceful. Kagawa visited them daily as they sat outside the docks, in the manner of strikers all over the world, watching their work but refusing to do it. He opened consumers' co-operatives which sold food and clothing at prices they could afford. He went day by day to the managers and ship-owners pleading the cause of the workers. Not unnaturally they refused to admit that there was any justice in his cause. The law was on their side and they intended to stand by it. Strikes were illegal. So were Unions. This was Japan, not America. If he persisted in going on they would have him arrested as an agitator.

This last was far from easy. He was preaching non-violence, not riot. There was a growing movement towards the organization of labour throughout the country, and both sides had to be temperate in their actions if they were not to alienate public opinion, which was quite undecided about these new industrial issues.

'Labourers are human beings,' proclaimed Kagawa in a manifesto. 'They are not to be bought and sold. . . . They are not machines. In order to develop our own personalities, to secure a social order which will produce true culture and give security, we demand the right to organize and regulate our own affairs.'

This was revolutionary. Common men had never spoken in this way before. It was clear that they had a leader of whom the country would have to take notice, now and in the future. The power of his leadership was seen in his ability to control the strikers as much as in his readiness to speak for them. When police and soldiers were called in to drive them back to work, there was real danger of a full-scale riot. Kagawa, small, slim and quiet, dealt with the police and quelled the agitators in his own ranks.

Foolishly, as it turned out, the police decided to end the strike by arresting its leader. Kagawa was followed by detectives. His hut and the labour headquarters were raided, and finally he himself was dragged away to the police-station, his clothes almost torn from his body and his face and back beaten with a policeman's sabre. Violence is an unwise weapon to use against a pacifist. Kagawa asked for an apology—and got it. Handcuffed, without shoes, he was thrust before the magistrate—who had no option but temporarily to hold him for investigation but spoke in high terms of his character. In the prison, his gentleness made a great impression both on warders and prisoners alike. To avoid the uneasiness of guarding a highly popular prisoner, he was transferred to the women's prison, but the women prisoners set about mending his clothes, and he was finally committed to a solitary cell. Even here, his spirit was unconfined.

> *Around my prison*
> *Runs a high stockade;*
> *And from my wrists*
> *Chains dangle;*
> *But no power*
> *Can lock my eyes.*

Dragging my chains,
I climb
To the tall window-ledge;
And though
My body cannot crawl
Between those grim iron rods,
Still can I
Laugh as my spirit flies
Into the purple skies!

Northward and Northward,
Up and up,
Up to the world of light
I go bounding;
Farewell, O Earth, farewell,
What need I now of your freedom?

Fearless, I fly and fly,
On through the heavenly sky;
Breaking all prison bars,
My soul sleeps with the stars!

In his mind, with only scraps of paper and some charcoal for material, he worked out the plot of a new novel, *Listening to the Voice in the Wall*.

Outside, his wife Haru had taken full charge of the two dispensaries, provided meals for the dozen or more 'lodgers' still living with them, read hundreds of letters which dealt with her husband's many activities, dictated replies, and consulted with the labour leaders day by day. Outside, too, other things were happening less in line with Kagawa's hopes. Communist elements in the docks were trying to gain control of the new union and planning a mass demonstration in which irreparable damage would be done to the shipyards. *That*, they insisted, would teach the shipowners who were the real masters.

67

After thirteen days, news leaked out that Kagawa was to be released. A thousand labourers gathered at the prison gate in the early evening, carrying banners of welcome and lighted lanterns hitched on the end of long poles. Fearing that the demonstration might result in their hero being kept in prison, the leaders urged the men to disperse, but they refused to go farther than the courtyard of a local temple, and there they waited until Kagawa did, indeed, emerge from the prison gates. Then, with a tumultuous welcome, they escorted him back home to Shinkawa.

The welcome was deceptive. Kagawa hoped it meant that the workers were prepared to abstain from violence. Instead, the following morning, he heard that a mass of labourers was marching to the ship-yards, led by the Communist agitators, with the hope of destroying the machinery, breaking up the ships and damaging the cargoes. Rushing from the house, he ran as fast as he could towards the docks. There was only one place at which they might be halted— a narrow bridge which they must cross to reach the docks. For all he knew, they might already have passed it. Panting and almost doubled up with the tearing pain in his lungs, Kagawa reached the bridge and held on to it for support. In the distance he could hear the shouts of the marching army.

'O God, let there be peace!' He had neither energy nor coherent thought for more than that short prayer. Then, while he still struggled for breath, the strikers were on him. He held up his hand, and they stopped. A sick man, weakened by a fortnight on prison rations, dressed in the same seven-and-sixpenny labourer's suit which the strikers themselves habitually wore, he talked to them of peace and negotiation. Slowly, swayed by the power of his personality rather than his words, the men at the back moved away. Others joined them, until the stream became a river.

Deserting their Communist leaders and cheering Kagawa, the strikers dispersed.

Nothing could more effectively have proved his case with the employers. Peaceful negotiations were initiated. The existence of the Trades Union was admitted and accepted. New conditions of labour were agreed. Toyohiko Kagawa was a name known all over Japan. But as he spoke to the labourers, he left them in no doubt of his own position. 'Unions are necessary—but labour problems can only be solved by a change in the heart of the labourer himself!'

CHAPTER SEVEN

Earthquake in Tokyo

ABOVE THE rooftops of Kobe, beyond the Ikuta river, rose the green slopes of Mount Rokko. Now and again, especially in the earlier, less busy days, Kagawa had crossed the Higurashi bridge, made his way out of the town, and climbed from the degradation of Shinkawa to the refreshing solitude of the mountain. From its heights he could look down on the fields, where the rice grew vividly green against the muddy brown irrigation water, or out to the sea, silver and blue below him.

In Tokyo, he had been as much stirred by the lonely, mystical beauty of holy Mount Fujiyama as any Buddhist pilgrim who set out to gain merit by climbing to the summit. From the Labour Office, as from the prison, his mind sped to the clear atmosphere of the countryside and the loveliness of the land he loved so much.

Japan is a lovely country, mountainous throughout, with a long indented coast-line studded with islands and land-locked bays. In spring-time, when the valleys are ethereal with plum and almond blossom and the bright blue skies are flecked with white clouds, no land in the world can be more beautiful. Kagawa, despite his immersion in the town, was a countryman.

'This civilization of steel and concrete separates man from the soil,' he wrote. 'The soil is God's footstool. The scent of the soil heals me. I have no desire to become a civilized

70

man. I want to live close to the soil.' So he set down his longings in his *Meditations*. But he was a realist as well as a lover of beauty. He knew well enough that those who lived close to the soil were poor, under-fed, sick and without even the common rights of town-dwellers. He had lived long enough in Awa, and travelled sufficiently about the country in the past years, to see that it was the poverty of the country which drew hungry men and women to the false security of the towns, and left them in the squalor of the slums. His investigations into the causes of poverty sent him time and again into the country, and left him convinced that if Japanese poverty were to be attacked at the source it would have to be a battle on a double front, rural as well as urban.

In 1921, he invited seventy-two people from all over Japan to meet him in Shinkawa to talk over the problems of the country-dwellers. Much that they set down in that meeting was remarkable, but the most astonishing thing of all, to the visitors, was Kagawa's own encyclopedic and detailed knowledge of the situation. They knew already that natural resources were limited, but Kagawa pointed out how restricted they really were, and what were the effects of it.

'Eighty-two per cent. of Japan is mountainous, and only 18 per cent. is properly cultivable. Half the cultivated lands are rice-fields. There is not enough interest or knowledge to plant anything else.

'Small-holdings average only one and a half acres. Two million tenant-farmers have holdings that are only a little more than an acre each. These tenant-farmers have to hand over from 50 per cent. to 70 per cent. of their earnings to the landlords. Ten thousand of them go bankrupt every year.

'A hundred thousand young people come to the towns

every year—and many of them end up in the slums. Even then they are better off than those who stay behind. The death rate is higher in the villages than anywhere else in the Empire. We have a million people suffering from tuberculosis in Japan, and the majority of them live in the good, clear air of the country.'

The visitors waited. 'What can we do?' asked one, breaking the silence.

Kagawa's face brightened with enthusiasm. 'We must do the same as we have done here amongst the dock-labourers. We must form a Union.'

'But Unions are illegal—and it's easier for a landlord to turn out his tenants than it is for a ship-owner to dismiss a workman.'

'Japan,' asserted Kagawa, 'is becoming a great nation. She knows she can only keep her place in the modern world by thinking in modern terms. Unions, guilds, whatever you like to call them, are inevitable.'

'Even agricultural unions?'

The reformer nodded. 'Certainly.' He went on to expound his plans. Before the representatives dispersed, the first Agricultural Union of Japan had been organized. The issuing of a magazine, *The Soil and Freedom*, was agreed upon, with Kagawa, almost inevitably, adding the editing of it to his other multitudinous tasks.

Later that same year, the first All-Japan Peasant Conference was held, and the Japan Peasants' Union launched. Its manifesto bore in every phrase the mark of Kagawa's attitude to life. 'We purpose to nourish knowledge, improve our technique, cultivate our moral character, bring the element of enjoyment into life on the farm, and make the realization of a perfect rural civilization our goal. Standing for freedom of thought and assuming an attitude which will benefit society as a whole, we will love the truth. In order to realize an emancipation void of compromise, we will fight capitalism by organizing producer's guilds, and attain the liberation of the poverty-suffering peasant.' Kagawa was standing squarely on the Socialist platform, declaring war on capitalism. The Union caused a sensation because it immediately turned its high-sounding phrases into action. It decided to assist in cases of disputes between landlords and tenants, to contest the forthcoming elections on behalf of the peasant party, to promote laws for the protection of tenant-farmers, and to strive for the nationalization of land.

If Kagawa's socialism was evident in the manifesto, so were his vehement belief in life as a gift of God meant to be enjoyed, and his deep sense of corporate responsibility. Tenants had no more right to the advantages of the land than had their almost feudal landlords unless they worked hard and productively. Village industries needed reviving, new methods must be applied to agriculture and more initiative brought to the production of a wider variety of crops. An office was set up to advise on these matters, with Kagawa in general control.

Despite the antagonism of the landlords, as well as the industrialists, and his occasional arrest by irritated authorities, Toyohoki Kagawa at the age of thirty-three was an acknowledged leader in rural reform, a man of influence in industrial disputes and a major figure in contemporary Japanese literature.

> *I shall not say*
> *That I am busy—*
> *Those who would help*
> *The troubled people*
> *Should expect to be*
> *Busy always.*

Christ was so thronged
By multitudes
He had no time to eat.
He said,
'To him that hath
Shall be given;
And from him that hath not
Shall be taken away
Even that
He seems to have.'
Which means
That if we do not use
All of our powers
We lose them.

This also
We must not forget—
System, which gets work done!
Then, too, the problem is
To do our work
With all our hearts;
We do not tire
Of doing what we love.

But most of all,
Our strength and comfort come
Only when God
Dwells in our souls
Working together with us.

The year 1922 brought changes to the Kagawa household. After eight years of marriage their first child, a boy whom they named Sumimoto, was born. Two girls were to follow later, after the family's removal to Tokyo—Chiyoki and Umeko. The rhythm of life was altered. The

a deep-sea fishing vessel, sailed up the coast to Tokyo, and immediately set about establishing relief centres. Very soon mission authorities sent help and workers, Christian friends in Tokyo came to his assistance, and the Government really saw him at work. In such an emergency his shrewd ability to plan details while he thought in far broader terms came into full play.

Then the seemingly impossible happened. An Imperial Economic Commission was set up by the Government, with the Prime Minister as chairman. It consisted of a hundred and eighty members—government officials, commercial magnates such as the directors of petroleum, shipping and coal companies, and high-grade civil servants. Because of his intimate knowledge of the conditions under which the poor lived and his association with the labouring classes, Kagawa was invited to join the Commission. He was the only man chosen from the ranks of the people, and there were not a few on the Commission against whom he had fought in the labour troubles of the previous few years. So that there might be no dissension in the Commission over the main issue for which it had been set up, Kagawa publicly proclaimed a truce with the authorities over labour questions. As a result, he was able to concentrate on the rehabilitation and rebuilding schemes, and in the end the plans which were promulgated owed a great deal to his genius. To suggest that the final schemes were entirely his own and that, in every particular, the Commission was won to his point of view would be absurd, but in fact something more far-reaching happened in the many meetings and sub-committees of the planning authorities. They came to recognize Kagawa's sincerity, his intimate knowledge of the people whom they themselves hardly knew, his astonishing familiarity with the whole realm of economic theory and its practical application in other countries, and the quality of mystical Christianity which shone through everything he said and did.

Largely because of his urgent pressure, an Anti-Exploitation Land Act was made law, making it impossible for speculative landlords to withhold land which the Government wished to purchase for productive purposes. In addition he found himself appointed to serve on other Government Commissions—on unemployment, the organization of Labour Exchanges and emigration. By 1925, the law against Trades Unions was repealed, and permission was given for labour to organize itself on the commonly-accepted union basis of other countries.

His greatest triumph came in 1926. During his stay in Tokyo he had made nation-wide tours speaking about the slums, and had written hundreds of thousands of words about them, including a sequel to *Across the Death-line*. The long years in the squalor of Shinkawa were to have their result. Other reformers joined in his protests. If it was right to house the population of Tokyo in new blocks of flats and tenements, then it was manifestly wrong to leave other slum-dwellers in misery merely because they had not suffered the horrors of earthquake and fire. At last, three years after Kagawa came to the capital and began to associate with the main figures of Government, a law was passed which put an end to the slums. A six-year plan was initiated, and £2,000,000 appropriated, for destroying the overcrowded areas of Osaka, Kobe, Kyoto, Nagoya and what was left of Tokyo and Yokohama, and rehousing the tens of thousands of people who lived there. It was an Act which vindicated the Christian reformer's faith and the self-abnegation of his chosen life in the slums.

Soon after he had been appointed to serve on the Government Commission he decided to move to Tokyo. It would be impossible to work from Kobe, and in any case the time was opportune for him to live and plan at the centre of Japanese official, educational, social and Christian life. Leaving their new house at Nishinomiya, he bought a small house on the outskirts of Tokyo for about £16. Here, on a 'do-it-yourself' basis, he furnished his home with cupboards, tables, bookshelves and other furnishings made from packing-cases and any usable pieces of wood which he found available. Like all Japanese homes, it was never cluttered with furniture. The floor was used for sitting and sleeping, and on it they knelt to eat their simple meals from low tables in the traditional way of all Japan. To have little in the way of furnishings was not the disability it might seem in the West. The grace and charm of parents and children seemed all the greater in the uncrowded rooms. On the other hand, the lack of small but expensive luxuries found in many comparable families was evidence of the lack of money to spend on them.

In one sense, Toyohiko and Haru Kagawa were not poor. Indeed, to those who knew how great was the sale of his books, Kagawa must have seemed rich as well as influential. The truth was that almost all he earned he gave away or used for one or other of his many schemes.

While he was working alongside the Government in planning the reconstruction of Tokyo, he was also beginning his own rehabilitation settlements and training-centres for urban and rural workers and leaders. These settlements, which included Bible training-centres, churches and kindergarten schools, he established in Kobe, Osaka and Tokyo. They were under his own control and oversight, and were to continue in existence until the coming of the Second World War. Much of his earnings went into the building and staffing of these settlements.

His allowance for family expenses he worked out at £8 per month. His children must share the experiences of the poor rather than the rich, and as they reached the age at which other teen-agers had gay clothes, cycles and jewellery, they found that neither rebellion nor persuasion would gain such things for themselves. Royalties from his books, even in the 1930's, brought him more than £2,000 a year. Kagawa resolutely refused to use it for himself, his family or his home. It was his only that it might be used for others, as the following typical story shows.

Mr Okamura was the secretary of the YMCA in Kobe. Meeting Kagawa, he told him that he was in considerable difficulty. There were bills that could not be paid and work that ought to be done, but the branch was desperately short of money.

'How much do you need?'

Mr Okamura calculated, his face full of depression, and named a sum. 'We have so many opportunities, but we can't take them without money.'

Kagawa put his hand into the pocket of his thin workman's suit and drew out a piece of paper. 'Take this,' he said.

Opening it, the YMCA man found it to be a cheque for the equivalent of £1,000, enclosed in a publisher's letter. It was payment for a new book, and Kagawa had received it only that morning.

'My dear Dr Kagawa, I couldn't possibly take it!'

'You must.' The tone was quite firm.

'But, Sensei, it's yours. You've earned it. It must have taken you months to write this book.'

Mr Okamura took the cheque at last, wishing he had never spoken of his need. In a letter he tried to dissuade his friend from such generosity. 'You shouldn't give money away like that,' he wrote.

Kagawa's reply was simple, and expressed much of his religious philosophy. 'Why shouldn't I? When your friend is dying, there is only one thing to do—give him your life-blood.'

CHAPTER EIGHT

One Million Christians

BY THE AGE of forty, Kagawa's name was becoming known throughout the Christian world. Exactly what he had done or what he stood for, however, was not so clear. Articles presented him to magazine-readers as a simple, good man who had gone to live in the slums so that he could 'help people'. A few of his books were becoming available outside Japan. Biographies, in English and continental European languages, began to appear, though they were not always accurate in either their descriptions of his philosophy or even the facts of his life. He was 'a great Christian' living in a strange land which he had only once left for a brief period of study in the United States. His name was becoming known. The man himself remained obscure. William Axling's shattering biography was not published until 1930.

It is difficult to think ourselves back into the 1920's. A great war, fought to end war, had exacerbated national hostilities instead of destroying hatred. The plenty which ought to have come with peace had, in many places, turned into poverty. Labour troubles and disputes followed on the heels of unemployment. The international peace organization, the League of Nations, had been weakened, if not paralysed, by the refusal of the United States to accept membership in it, and was already showing itself incapable of facing major issues, though it dealt with a large number of smaller ones. In all this, the attentions of Europe and

America were largely fixed on themselves. Asia and Africa remained remote. How remote is indicated by the fact that popular radio was still in its infancy and a woman thrilled the world by a solo flight from Britain to Australia which took about three weeks. To the popular mind, even in the Churches, the 'natives' of these two continents were still more than a little odd. Even missionary enthusiasts were still brought up on the stories of Mary Slessor of Calabar and the horrors of the Chinese Boxer Rebellion. True, there was a 'Chinatown' in many of the large ports, Japanese shopkeepers had settled in America, and Indian pioneers from the Punjab hawked silks from door to door in Britain, but fiction-writers and irritable mothers used these strange people as horrifics. They were nearby samples of far away strangers, exotic in the imagination but frightening at close quarters. The common appeal in annual missionary meetings in many places was to send the gospel to 'the heathen in his blindness who bows down to wood and stone'. There were few people who had even begun to think in terms of a World Church.

Part of Kagawa's significance at this time was that he was not only a Christian in a land where there were still comparatively few Christians; he was a Christian leader— and a leader from Asia. When a Western Church-member was asked at that period to name a great Christian African he would immediately speak of Aggrey. When he was asked to name a world-famous Christian from India, China, South-East Asia or Ceylon he was hard put to it to think of one. But, in a period when for the first time the old conception of missions was beginning to break down and the fact of 'the Church' was beginning to emerge, Toyohiko Kagawa was visible proof in flesh and blood and written word that the missionary lands had something to give as well as much to take. He was one of the first exciting evidences of the contribution which the Younger Churches, not yet dignified by that undignified name, had to make to the Christian heritage of the modern world.

In 1928 he visited the United States, but this time he went not as a poor and unknown student who had had to borrow his fare from his relatives and his missionary sponsors. Now, though he still chose to travel light and cheaply, unhampered by more than a suitcase, he went as a man of some consequence. Japan was closer to America than it was to Britain. Their interests in the Pacific, in trade and commerce, had much in common, and it was natural for these reasons, as well as because of his missionary links with the American Church, that Kagawa should turn to the United States for his first great preaching and lecturing tour. He received a traditionally generous American welcome. Travelling widely, preaching in many States, meeting influential Christian leaders, he continued his investigations into social conditions wherever he went. In Canada, he was given a much deserved Doctorate of Divinity. When he returned to Japan, it was with the comforting knowledge that in the United States and Canada he was regarded as a great and progressive thinker.

He needed such strength as his growing international reputation could give him, for in Japan there was no little suspicion and hostility. Sadly, a good deal of this was found in the Christian Church itself. Business men disliked his avowed socialism, which cut across their profit-making commercial interests. Denominational leaders were irritated by his lack of sectional loyalty and his unconventional view of the Church. Fundamentalist Churchmen complained that he was not sufficiently evangelical.

It is true that he was out of step with his Christian contemporaries in Japan. The mere fact that he was a novelist and poet of high repute was strange to many of them; his pacifism, in a land where a new militarist spirit was beginning to creep into society, made him suspect; but above all, his criticism of the Church robbed him of support—and sometimes he criticized it very sharply. The most outstanding instance of this was when he was invited in 1927, the year before he went to America, to address a national Conference of Religion. Buddhists had made the best claims they could for their own faith. Shinto was proclaimed as the natural religion of the people. Kagawa was expected to speak strongly in favour of Christianity. It was natural that he should do so, for with all his apparent ecclesiastical eccentricities, he was a deeply committed Christian. Instead, amidst the representatives of non-Christian faiths, he denounced the Church for its narrowness, its pietism and its leaders' complacent disregard of social and economic evils.

'I speak English very badly,' he said, at this period. 'When I say "denomination" some people think I am saying "damnation". I'm not surprised. To me, they are very much the same thing.'

His criticism was not for effect. No one was ever less of an exhibitionist. He spoke from conviction that the Church was failing the land he loved. Denominational rivalry, arguments about biblical interpretation and church-centred Christianity all seemed to him to miss the real point of the faith he held so dearly. Though he no longer lived in the slums, though indeed they were being swept away by the storm of protest he had aroused, his concern was with people, and especially the poor, the unprivileged, the sick and the young. Only by clothing the naked, visiting the prisoners, sharing his cup of cold water with those who had nothing could he fulfil the law of Christ. If the Church would not do these things, he at least must do so even if his activities alienated much of the sympathy which he longed to gain for his work. And fortunately, despite the hostility of conventional and conservative groups, there was a growing number of men and women, especially amongst the younger Church members and progressive thinkers in touch with Christian action in other countries, who supported him staunchly.

It was natural to him to interpret the compassion of Jesus in twentieth-century terms, and especially in the terms of Christian socialism. In 1922 he had founded the 'Friends of Jesus', a society almost Franciscan in conception, whose members were dedicated to the service of the unprivileged, and who accepted purity, peace, piety, labour and service-ableness as the guiding principles of their lives. In 1925, after coming to Tokyo and finding the disabilities under which students had to live, with little money to spare even for necessities, he founded students' co-operative societies. The co-operative system, under which shops sold essentials to members without profit, was something he had already pioneered amongst farmers, dock-labourers and factory workers. Clothes, books, food, tools and many other necessary commodities became available at low prices through the co-operatives. In the same serviceable spirit, he began hostels for students and working men in Tokyo, Osaka and Kobe. Almost all these ventures were revolutionary, and though Kagawa refused to become committed to any political party, they had a certain political significance.

'I am not,' he said, 'a Christian because I am a Socialist. I am a Socialist because I am a Christian.' Nor, because he had become a man of consequence with an income reckoned in several thousands of pounds a year from his literary work, did he turn into a wealthy director of reform who paid others to exercise Socialism on his behalf. In the slums he had written a poem which was a cry from the heart.

Penniless. . . .
A while
Without food
I can live;
But it breaks my heart
To know
I cannot give.

Penniless. . . .
I can share my rags,
But I—
I cannot bear to hear
Starved children cry.

Penniless. . . .
And rain falls,
But trust is true.
Helpless, I wait to see
What God will do.

Now that he was no longer penniless he could see what God had done. In Shinkawa he had been the friend and servant of eleven thousand people. But Japan was only Shinkawa repeated over and over again, in need if not in pattern. There were 30,000,000 farm-workers and country-dwellers, 5,000,000 industrial workers, 1,500,000 fishermen, 1,000,000 transport workers, 1,000,000 in the Public Works Department of the Government, 500,000 miners. They were as much in need as the people he had lived close to in Kobe. The 'helpless' mood of his heart-stricken poem had been swept away. Waiting to see what God would do had brought him a clear answer. Through the gifts of literary skill and money, the power of speech and the friendship of men in high places, God had given him a responsibility for Japan's forty million under-privileged people.

Opposition and criticism were small obstacles compared with the greatness of the task and the opportunity which lay to his hand.

Because of the misunderstanding which so easily clings about his reputation, it is necessary to assert both sides of Kagawa's character—his belief in Christian action and his profound spiritual awareness.

'He has an almost instinctive understanding of the Bible,' wrote one friend.

'I know of no man I have ever met who so possessed the mind of Christ,' wrote a missionary.

'No modern Christian has ever taken the Sermon on the Mount quite so literally,' said a third.

Much of his mysticism can be illustrated from his own words and writings. 'I am a man of prayer. Naturally, there are times when I ponder whether from the standpoint of philosophy it is a good or a bad thing to pray. But I do not pray because it is philosophically the thing to do. I pray because I am a living being.'

Like all the great Christians, his emphasis has been on holiness—not merely holiness of outward living but of the heart. 'The aspiration for holiness . . . this is the very heart of religious living. When one is charmed by the Holy One and as a captive of the Holy of Holies offers himself up as a mass on God's altar, morals become a festival and religion becomes a sweet-scented perfume rising Godward. Holiness is the heavenward open window of the soul. Holiness is the well God has dug down into a man's spirit. . . . There is but one straight path to holiness. There must be no winding hither and thither. This path is known only to the sanctified whose faces are set toward the supreme domain.'

Naturally, the centre of his thinking concerns love. 'There is no revelation but love. God should not be sought for in books, nor in the organization of institutions. God should not be looked for theoretically, but God should be loved. God reveals himself only in love. . . . Love awakens all it touches. Love whispers to the ear and arouses the heart. . . . Creation is an ornament designed by love. . . . For love, everything that exists is a victory. Everything is created for love's sake. Love is alpha and omega, the beginning and the ending. Love is the true nature of God. The sanctuary of God is love. I know that I can worship God only in love. All the idols and the temples and cathedrals are nothing but symbols. I worship God only in love. All forms and ceremonies are but supplements.'

'Jesus Christ is the greatest educator in the world—a teacher of love.'

To Kagawa, Jesus Christ has never been a subject for theological argument. He would have found it possible to worship God, in love, even without the revelation of Jesus. But, to him, one of the supreme elements of Christ's revelation of the character of God has always been that of compassion. He cannot speak of his love for Jesus without seeing the demands such love must make on the Christian.

> *As in a single Word, Christ's Love-Movement*
> *Is summed up in the Cross. The Cross is*
> *The whole of Christ, the whole of Love.*
> *God speaks to man through the Cross,*
> *Of love's mysteries concealed in the divine bosom.*
>
> *Leave to the Greeks their theories of divinity!*
> *Abandon to their musty libraries those scholars*
> *Who fail to love humanity. . . .*
>
> *Is your love-citadel completed, friends?*
> *Have you entered into your rightful inheritance*
> *Of death to self and service to others?*

Have you done your portion of road-breaking
For the way of the Cross—among the lepers,
Among the tuberculous, among the aborigines of Formosa,
Or along the ice-bound straits of the Northern Seas?
Without the Cross there is no victory!

No one could do all these things. But every man and woman who loved God, and saw God in Christ, must do some of them.

> *. . . In the blood-drops dripping*
> *Along the sorrowful road to the Via Dolorosa*
> *Will be written the history of man's regeneration.*
> *Tracing those blood-stained and staggering footprints*
> *Let me go forward!*
> *This day also must* my *blood flow, following*
> *In that blood-stained pattern.*

For Kagawa, the words were almost literally fulfilled. He shed his own life-blood without care. He was thin, physically frail, and drove himself to the limit of physical endurance. Free though he was of tuberculosis, he was never free of the weakness that had resulted from it, and his lungs often brought him to the edge of pneumonia. His eyesight was not only impaired; one eye was completely blind, and the sight of the other was not good. There were many of his closest friends who did not believe he could stand the pace at which he was living, and yet, far from slowing up, he seemed to crowd more into each day as the years went by. In many cases, the early years of great men are crowded with incident, and the chief interest centres in their period of development and achievement. After that, the story settles into an almost monotonous pattern of places visited, speeches made and offices held. In Kagawa's case, every year, right to the end of the story, was one of interest and changing incident, and yet every day, as well as every year, was pierced and held by the same thread of Christian compassion.

Pacifism was one aspect of this compassion. He could never believe that war was right, or that the way to international or social peace could be found through violence. In 1927, a manifesto against military conscription was presented to the League of Nations. It was signed by such men as Romain Rolland, Einstein, Tagore, Gandhi. The only Japanese name was that of Kagawa—and it singled him out as a potential enemy of the militarists whose power was growing in Japan. They had always known this, but his action gave them an opportunity of denouncing him in public as a danger to the State. A year later, he gave them a new chance of holding him up to ridicule by founding and organizing the National Anti-War League of Japan. It was joined by leading figures in all the political parties as well as in literary, religious and social movements. To oppose war and preparations for it, to denounce aggression against weaker groups and peoples, was to ask for trouble, especially in the years when Japan was preparing for her all-out attack on China.

'Burn him! Burn Kagawa! Kagawa is a traitor! Kagawa is in the pay of the American imperialists! Kagawa is the tool of the Russian Communists!' These phrases, and others like them, were repeated over and over again in the newspapers controlled by the Japanese nationalists and in pamphlets broadcast, particularly in the towns, by those whose interests he opposed.

He was in China, a country which had good reason to fear the militarist intentions of Japan, when the great vision of this period of his life came to him. He had been reading the history of the Huguenot Movement in France, and was impressed with the way it had spread. In his mind, too, was the concept of 'mission' as part of the Church, for he was due to go to Jerusalem to attend the International Missionary Council there. Japan needed more Christians, more men and women committed to carrying their faith into every part of life. The 300,000 Protestant Christians, the result of seventy years of Protestant missions, would all have agreed with that statement—and yet the Church grew almost imperceptibly when it should have spread like a fire through the forests in summer-time. As he thought in this way, a single phrase rang in his mind: 'One million Christians!'

It was possible. It must surely be God's will to extend His Kingdom. The Church itself was the stumbling-block, uncommitted as it was to the idea of 'mission', or so it seemed to Kagawa. Within an hour or so, in his mind though not in any organized way, the 'Kingdom of God Movement' was born.

He went to Jerusalem, to be moved to the depths both by walking in the footsteps of his Master and by mingling with Christian leaders from all over the world. To talk about 'missions' in Jerusalem, however, was pointless unless Church leaders were prepared to put their ideas to the test when they were at home. He returned to Tokyo to spend much of the next eighteen months advocating the 'Kingdom Movement' up and down Japan.

Aware though he was that the Kingdom does not come either by looking for it or by holding committees, he had spent much of his life planning and knew the value of careful organization. After consulting friends, mission groups and preachers in many denominations during 1929, he formed a Central Committee in 1930 despite the opinion of many whom he talked with that his idea was impractical and impossible. During the same year ninety Regional Committees were set up and a publication, *The Kingdom of God Newspaper*, made its appearance. Within a couple of years its circulation was over 30,000 copies.

In all this Kagawa's aim was simple. He coveted the people of Japan for Christ. The Kingdom of God Movement was a daring, nation-wide evangelistic campaign. It was also a convincing answer to those who complained that he was first of all a Socialist and only secondarily a Christian minister.

The year 1930 was a desperate one in Japan. Tokyo had been hit hard by the earthquake seven years earlier, but now the whole country began to feel the effects of the slump which was affecting both East and West. In the United States the depression was to result in the catastrophic collapse on Wall Street. In Britain unemployment figures rose to the highest figure ever recorded, with skilled technicians and highly trained executives joining the ranks of the workless. In Japan, and especially in Tokyo, the situation was desperate. The unemployed slept out in the open during a winter of heavy rain and snow. The death-rate soared, from respiratory diseases, malnutrition and suicide. The corporation in Tokyo had set apart an annual sum of £1,000,000 for social relief and had eight hundred people working in the Social Welfare bureau, but the money seemed insufficient and the crowded department was increasingly ineffective if not downright inefficient. Custom forbade anyone other than permanent officials to be brought in at the top organizing level.

Mayor Horikira decided to break with civil service practice. Desperate need demanded an out-of-the-rut solution. He sent for Kagawa to come to see him at the City Hall.

'Dr Kagawa,' he said, 'I want you to help us.'

'I am doing all I can in my settlements with the resources I have.'

'It is not enough. Nothing we are doing is really meeting the situation. But your experience is exactly what we

need.' He took a deep breath. His proposal was unpre-
cedented, and even now he almost hesitated to put it. 'I
want you to become Chief of the Welfare Department.'

'But I'm not an official.'

'We must dispense with tradition. You are the man most
fitted in Tokyo for the work we have in mind—the best
qualified man in the country.'

'It would not work. You must promote someone else.
The Department wouldn't tolerate someone coming in
from outside.'

'The Department will accept what I say. It needs pulling
together, organizing, giving a sense of purpose. I am prepared to offer you a salary of £1,800 a year.'

'No!' Kagawa's voice was quite firm.

Mayor Horikira looked taken aback. 'It would support
your settlement work for a year, if you don't wish to take
it for yourself. But I can't go any higher. There is, of
course, an office, all the staff you need, and a car.'

Kagawa smiled gently. 'It isn't too little. It's too much.
If you want me, I will help. But I can't become an official
and take over the Chief's job. I have too many commit-
ments in the Church just now. But,' he reiterated, 'if you
wish me to help, I will agree to become Chief Adviser,
without salary of any kind, and spend ten days a month
in the service of the Welfare Department.'

It was quixotic in the extreme, but the decision matched
Kagawa's whole attitude to service as something to be given
freely and without personal gain. The Chief of the Department was removed. Kagawa became, in effect, the king-
pin on which the whole welfare of Tokyo moved. He was
met at the station by an official car which took him to the
City Hall—an arrangement he agreed to because it made
his work more expeditious—and he took his place at the
big desk and toured the distressed areas of the city. That

he had turned down a huge salary and chose to work in his normal, working-man's 'seven-and-sixpenny suit' gave point to the work he set out to do.

The programme he carried through, with the co-operation of the Department, and the reluctant support of those in the Corporation who criticized his socialist attitude, was immense. He began by visiting every place in which there was distress. Then, with a clear picture of what was needed, he set to work. First, he secured shelter for the homeless. Then he tackled the problem of the 31,000 boatmen who lived in six-by-nine-foot shacks on Tokyo's two hundred miles of canals, getting them housed and making provision for the education of their children. Because the unemployed needed work as well as relief, he carried through the opening of eleven new social settlements in the worst-hit areas of the city. Provision was made for decent, city-aided burial for the dead, so that a proper respect could find its way into family life again. Within a few months, he had brought in a scheme for unemployment benefit and insurance, matched by a demand that the unemployed should take work when it was offered to them. Available work was distributed as equally as possible amongst the unemployed. Graft and corruption had no place in his administration. Gradually, under his ten-day-per-month leadership, the depression was met and the situation changed for the better.

What about the other twenty days each month? Here, once more, was Kagawa's answer to those who suggested that he was deserting the work of the Christian ministry for the tougher, more spectacular sphere of social service.

The Kingdom of God Movement was touching the whole country, rural areas as well as towns. The ninety regional committees were hard at work organizing campaigns. Wherever the Movement was at work, Kagawa was there. Wherever it was slow to take action, Kagawa was there too, to stimulate and encourage. At one time, six campaigns were going on simultaneously. Kagawa was engaged in every one of them, travelling from one place to another so that he might speak at them all. Though he had never been more deeply involved in social service, he had never done more preaching. The central theme of his preaching was the Cross of Christ as the revelation of the love of God. And wherever he preached, with his words coming to life because of his own practical compassion, men heard the voice of God. Not in ones and twos, but in dozens and scores, they came into the Kingdom of God.

CHAPTER NINE

Japan Prepares for Conquest

ONE OF THE results of the Russo-Japanese War, which had caused Kagawa to throw down his rifle in the drill class at his high school in Kobe and declare himself a schoolboy pacifist, was that the Japanese were given the right to maintain some 15,000 soldiers in Manchuria. It was their duty to protect the South Manchurian Railway which ran from the Trans-Siberian Railway to the naval base of Port Arthur. To that extent the Japanese had had, for thirty years, a section of its army on soil adjacent to China. During those years, the Japanese imperialist group, led by militarists in the Government, had coveted the Chinese mainland, the size and potentialities of which were in such startling contrast to its own over-populated, non-productive islands. In September 1931 Japan accused China of having blown up part of the railway line at Mukden, north of Port Arthur. Immediately, the Japanese Army and Air Force went into action. The great natural and mineral resources of Manchuria offered rich supplies to a country which could exploit them, as China, at that time, had not begun to do.

At this period, though Mussolini was the acknowledged dictator of Italy, Hitler was only beginning his swift climb to power in Germany. The 'Manchurian Incident' was one of the first symptoms of the war-sickness which was to corrupt and almost destroy the world within a decade. It was against this background of violence that Kagawa was to spend a large part of his later life.

In 1931, towards the end of the year, he fulfilled a promise to go and lecture in Shanghai. He was deeply troubled about his country's action, and his reception was a mixture of coldness and hostility. The fact that he was a Christian mattered little to a nation which, itself, was not greatly touched by the Christian faith, and there was talk of forbidding him to lecture. Though this did not happen, the threat of physical violence was seldom absent in his first days in Shanghai. He himself, however, went on with his work almost as if he were unaware of the animus against him. At home, in addition to all the supervisory work he undertook in connection with his settlements, his involvement in Tokyo reconstruction and his evangelistic tours, he continued the editorship of newspapers and magazines. In one of these periodicals, *The Friends of Jesus Magazine*, there appears a long outline of his lectures in Shanghai which shows clearly, not only his approach to the Christian life, but also his immense breadth of interest and knowledge.

The subject of his lectures to crowded classes of students was his most familiar choice, the Cross of Christ. Nowhere would it be possible to find lectures on this subject less pietistic, coldly theological or emotionally introspective.

The first study was 'The Cross as the Foundation of Social Evolution'. Much of it is given over to an examination of Marxist principles, and he sets against them the discipline, inwardness, selflessness and purpose of the Cross. To him, however, it is being false to Christ to neglect the material facts of life. The sharing of the Cross involves the Christian in self-denial. To Kagawa, the great touchstone of the doctrine of self-denial is food. 'I talked in an evangelistic campaign for thirty minutes about food,' he told his audience. 'Afterwards the Chairman said I was talking too much about food and too little about the Cross. I told him I never give an evangelistic address in Japan without talking about food. An economist has shown that the food problem of the world arises because most of us want delicacies instead of only necessities. This means a wrong use of money—a wrong idea of what it is for. When men have money they want more of it—and they always want it for the wrong reasons.' In the same lecture he attacks current ideas of sex and sexual morality, using the Cross of Christ to illuminate the selfishness of men.

His second study was on 'The Cross and the City Problem', and in this he spoke at length about the Co-operative Movement in which he was a Japanese pioneer. The third concerned 'The Cross and the Village Problem'. The problem was not to be solved only by an understanding of villagers' psychology and an encouragement to love the land, to love their neighbours and to love God. To accept the Cross, for a villager, involved such pieces of self-sacrifice as eating more pork instead of merely using pigs as scavengers, and breaking with tradition by stocking the village's lakes with different species of fish. Two other studies on Education, approached from the individual's gain from it and the social responsibilities of the educators —the last ranging through a series of sections dealing with the home, labour, the markets, efficiency, law and culture —completed a series of extraordinarily wide-ranging, theologically-based lectures which it must have been almost impossible for either students or professors fully to appreciate.

Indeed, it was not easy at times even for them to understand what he was saying. He was a Japanese, talking to Chinese. Because neither could understand the other's language, he spoke in English—a language with which he was brilliantly familiar on paper, but which he spoke awkwardly. A listener has described how he moved swiftly from one blackboard to another, talking as he moved, facing them or facing the audience, always without notes and always fully charged with emotion about the subject he was discussing. The boards were filled with the names of philosophers, theologians and scientists of all ages, and with economists and socialists from all over the twentieth-century world. There were lists of books—major works, all of them—in English, French and German—which would be accessible only in university libraries, and even then perhaps only in specialist ones. Philosophy, theology, sociology, economics, biology, history and personal holiness were called upon to illustrate the principles of love, self-sacrifice and authority seen in the Cross. None of this, however, was for the sake of mental exercise, but only to point them to the Cross which was the theme of his lectures and his preaching. The total effect this half-blind, inwardly illuminated speaker had on his audience was not one of learning. As one student put it afterwards: 'He left us feeling, as Jesus said before him, "I have food of which you know nothing"!'

One other thing he did, which put him in a category apart from any other Japanese of his time. As a preface to his lectures, and in the Tsinan issue of *The Friends of Jesus Magazine*, as well as in the Chinese churches where he preached, he apologized on behalf of the Christians in Japan for his country's 'attack' on Manchuria. He did not examine the alleged provocation behind the 'Manchurian Incident'. For him, war in any circumstance was wrong—and he knew well enough the expansionist designs his country had on China. He simply said, clearly and with tears in his eyes, that Japan's action was wrong. As one Japanese to the whole Chinese nation he apologized, and asked for forgiveness.

He did not grovel. His words are simple and sincere. But in Japan as in China, to admit wrong-doing and crave forgiveness is to 'lose face'. On 18th February 1932, when Japan had finally expelled the Chinese from Manchuria, the Japanese proclaimed the accession of a new State to the Japanese Empire, to which they gave the name Manchukuo. In those days of victory, Kagawa's action exacerbated the attitude of his critics. Pacifism was a theory which eccentric Christians might presumably hold if they wished; pacifism in action, when it humiliated the whole nation, was intolerable. From that moment, to some of the militarist cliques of Japan, Kagawa was an enemy to be destroyed.

He did not appear a very formidable enemy when he came back from his Chinese lecture tour. His eyes were giving him serious trouble, and, exhausted by the physical and emotional strains of the past months, he suddenly collapsed with pneumonia and a recurrence of his lung trouble. The doctors were insistent. He must give up all his work and rest for several months. For a week or two he obeyed their orders. The little house was quiet. Callers were kept at a distance by Haru Kagawa. Those who came in, leaving their wooden-soled sandals at the door, bent down to catch the mumbled words of the little man shifting painfully on the low bed, and then went about their business. The children, Sumimoto and his two sisters, Chiyoko and Umeko, suppressed their shrill chatter and their laughter, so natural to every Japanese child, and went out to join the small boys and girls in the kindergarten across the compound. The friends who called left with serious faces. The *Sensei* was evidently not merely suffering from one of his periodical attacks of illness. He had almost burned himself out.

Few men have more completely proved the ascendancy

of the human spirit over physical frailty. Within three weeks Kagawa was keeping four secretaries hard at work taking down dictation, making notes and typing. From his bed, obeying the doctor's orders not to get up but paying no attention to the spirit of his injunction, he was answering the scores of letters which arrived each day, dictating poems, articles and editorials for his own magazines and others to which he contributed, and making notes for the books he still hoped to write. From his bed he solved problems of policy which arose on the compound and in his three main settlements. The sandals clattered up to the door once more, the little house was thronged with people whose quiet voices combined to make the air hum with noise. Within six weeks he was not only out of bed, but out of the house, back at work and preaching.

It was at this time that he initiated yet another new movement. In *Brotherhood Economics*, where we almost hear the sound of his voice dictating, he wrote these words. 'As a captive of the missionary movement, I want to give a testimony. I owe much to the missionaries who came over to Japan from America.' He goes on to pay a tribute to Dr Myers, saying (rather curiously, but aptly enough in the context), 'I don't know what denomination he belonged to', but speaking of his love and understanding. Then he goes on.

'I do not like to use the terms "Foreign Missions" and "Home Missions". When I was invited to speak to the New York Missionary Council four years ago, I said: "It is necessary to change the names of the missionary boards. Look at the Russians, the Soviet people; they use the 'Third Internationale'. Why can we not use the term 'Christian Internationale'?

'Although we are divided as to skin-colour, difference of nationality and difference of language, we are still real

Christians. To be real Christians we must belong to Heaven first, then to our nation. I belong to God first, then to Japan; therefore everywhere I feel at home. You may think that your country belongs to you, but it belongs to God first.

'Because you are blessed [in America] Christ requires your devotion, your sacrifices for the cause of the Christian Internationale.'

He was careful to point out that the 'Christian Internationale' was not an organization. It had no officers or headquarters. It was a movement, an idea to challenge the thinking and giving of Christian people. Even so, it involved another bulletin, the starting of prayer groups in cities and villages in various countries, and endless correspondence. He envisaged a conference of like-minded Christians in Asia.

It was at this period, somewhat recovered from his illness, that he became not only a world-famous name, but an internationally recognized figure. He set out on world tours, leaving his Japanese ventures in the hands of his trusted friends. All he wrote in *Brotherhood Economics*, the printed form of lectures given at Colgate-Rochester Divinity School, New York, in 1936, was inspired by his sense of Christian internationalism. The practical application he gave to the Christian faith in his lectures at Shanghai was taken over and put in a world setting. Without any thought of personal fame or profit, he moved in and out of the great Christian centres of the world.

Between 1931 and 1936 he visited China, India, Australia, Europe and, once more, America. The irony of his world tours was that they established him as one of the major Christian figures of the twentieth century without achieving the one result he longed for—an international Christian standpoint. The great nations were prepared to agree that their economies needed overhauling, but not for the reasons he adduced. With industrial depression still not overcome, and the fear of war in Europe, pacifism was regarded as an intellectual oddity, unrelated to ordinary living. Economics must be geared to the production of more armaments. The Japanese reformer's assertion that economic reconstruction involved international brother-hood, the coming of the spirit of Jesus into industry and commerce, was no more than the inarticulate mumblings of a foreign Christian with his head in the sand. World peace, he insisted, could only be established on 'spiritu-alized' or 'brotherhood' economics. This sounded like non-sense to those who believed that it could only be guaranteed by larger national armed services and more destructive weapons. It was difficult to overlook the fact that he came from the only really aggressive nation in Asia, which had already seized Manchuria and was more than likely to pursue its imperialistic aims in China. Almost everywhere he went, however, his personal integrity was recognized and the quality of his thinking gave new impetus to progressive Christians who were capable of looking beyond their own national interests. The great exception to this was in America.

The United States had not recovered from the slump when he visited it in 1936. Communists, industrialists, and some of the Church leaders combined to use their influence to prevent his being allowed to land. When they failed, there was constant, bitter and ill-informed criticism in the Press. A clergyman held crowded meetings for a whole week to denounce him for his political ideas and his refusal to 'stick to evangelism'. In Los Angeles his meetings were broken up by Communists. To one who had always re-garded America as a second home it was an unhappy visit.

He was distressed but not despairing. In *Meditations on the Cross* he wrote: 'There are two kinds of Christianity—

success-Christianity and failure-Christianity. Jesus said, "Unless I fail, my work will be useless." It is, however, a fact that when anyone becomes a Christian there is the danger that he may become too successful! In contrast to this Jesus said a very gloomy thing; He said that He was intending to fail!'

His distress was for other people. In rejecting his words they were rejecting the hope of peace. Their rejection of himself meant only that he was sharing the Cross of Christ, the centre of his devotion as it was of his preaching. He returned to Japan in 1936 famous, disappointed and humble. True to his principles, he had refused to be fêted or to accept luxury in a world where so many lived in penury. Even on the ships he had deliberately chosen to travel in the lowest class—and there he had found peace.

> *Here on the broad Pacific,*
> *In the porthole passage, is my sanctuary,*
> *My suitcase on an orange box for a desk.*
> *Ah! The tropic summer heat*
> *In this my stifling room!*
> *But lo! this is the way to endless life*
> *If I but call this place my monastery!*

The suspicion, thrown into sharp relief by Kagawa's own gentleness, that Japan was as instinctively aggressive in Asia as were Germany and Italy in Europe was only too well founded. In 1933, when Germany was rearming in defiance of the Versailles Treaty, school-children were learning this poem by heart.

> *Great Japan, great Japan,*
> *We citizens, ninety millions of us,*
> *Humbly serve the Emperor,*
> *Looking up to him as god,*
> *Longing for him as a parent.*

Great Japan, great Japan,
Through all the ages
Never once defeated by the enemy,
The glory of our country
Will shine yet brighter and brighter
Like the sun and the moon.

A year before, the Conservative leaders Baron Dan, the Finance Minister Inouye and the Prime Minister Inukai had been assassinated, making way for more military-minded elements. In 1936, some two thousand soldiers staged a revolt in which the Finance Minister Takahishi, who had largely controlled the financial grants to the army, the Lord Privy Seal, Viscount Saito, and General Watanabe were murdered. At first it was believed that Premier Okada had also been killed, but it was found that by mistake his cousin who resembled him had been assassinated in his place. The rebellion was brought under control, but only at the expense of leaders who had a restraining influence on the Government's aggressive policies. In the same year, Japan withdrew from the League of Nations and from the London Naval Conference, and on 25th November signed the Anti-Comintern Pact with Germany—another sign of her long-maintained enmity with Russia.

To Kagawa, some of these were personal losses. When he first became associated with the Government, six of the Cabinet Ministers had wives who were Christians—a fact which accounted in no small measure for the tolerance of Government leaders. Now, those days were gone. Instead, with General Hayashi as its aggressively militarist Prime Minister, the Government revived the *Sai-sei-itchi* conception—'The unity of worship and Government'. Shinto, the worship of the Emperor as the incarnation of the Sun-god and the representative of the spirit of Japan, became widespread, and eventually compulsory. 'Bowing to the Emperor' began the day in school and office. To some, it had no more religious significance than singing the national anthem or saluting the flag in other countries. Christians tried to view it in this spirit. There is no doubt, however, that it was intended to have a more significant *mystique* and meaning than this. It was a semi-religious observance by which the nation would be bound together in whatever projects Emperor and Government decreed. It was a subtle attack on such internationally activated groups as the Christian Church, and prepared the way for the Religious Bodies Bill of 1939, which placed all religions under Government control.

On 7th July 1937 Japan declared war on China. The world was horrified as the news of this aggression was broadcast. America seemed to have convincing proof that pacifism did not pay. Europe began feverishly to rearm to withstand the growing 'territorial ambitions' of Hitler and Mussolini, who had already invaded Ethiopia on Good Friday, 1935. Chinese towns were bombed indiscriminately. Little more mercy was shown to civilians than to soldiers as the Japanese armies pressed forward, occupying town after town.

In Tokyo, Kagawa was more deeply stricken than he had ever been by his own distresses. He wept for China, for Japan, for the Church. He poured out his sorrow in a poem, *To Tears*.

> *Ah tears! Unbidden tears!*
> *Familiar friends since childhood's lonely years,*
> *Long separated we.*
> *Why do ye come again to dwell with me?*
>
> *At midnight, dawn, midday,*
> *Ye come; nor wait your coming, nor delay;*
> *Nay fearless, with what scorn,*
> *Ye picture China by my brothers torn.*

Your scorn I must accept,
But I'm no coward; pray heed ere more ye've wept;
I love Japan so fair,
And China too; this war I cannot bear.

'Is there no other way?'
Thus do I search my spirit all the day
Nor ever reach a goal;
I love, but only am a phantom soul.

Like Christ who bore our sins upon the Cross
I too must bear my country's sins and dross;
Land of my love! Thy sins are grievous to be borne,
My head hangs low upon my form forlorn.

The Japanese war in China, and the growing military character of the nation's economy, were darker blots on Japan than the slums had ever been. But even worse things were to come.

CHAPTER TEN

The Years of War

IN THE AUTUMN of 1938 representatives of the Churches and Missionary Societies in East and West made their way to Madras. Amongst the lovely buildings of the Christian College at Tambaram, bright with canna lilies and bougainvillea, the leaders of the Protestant world met and talked. 'Tambaram' was the successor of 'Edinburgh' and 'Jerusalem', the great ecumenical conferences of the International Missionary Council. Since Kagawa had gone to Jerusalem in 1928 there had been advances and regressions, triumph and disappointment. Atheist Communism was stronger than ever. In Europe, nationalism had produced the blasphemies of Hitlerism and the fascism of Mussolini. In Japan, nationalism implied a resurgence of old, totalitarian faiths. Yet, despite this beating back of Christianity, the Christian mission had been going forward in Asia and Africa. The phenomenon, as it seemed to some, of the change from 'mission' to 'Church' was seen to be the normal pattern of Christian history. For many who were at Tambaram, or read about it, the most significant feature of the Conference was the emergence of Christian leadership in what had long been regarded as 'missionary lands'. The necessity, as well as the strength, of this leadership in China and South-East Asia was to be demonstrated in the years that followed.

'Is there going to be war in Europe?' That, apart from all the theological questions which were debated at

Tambaram, was the query most often put to Western delegates.
It lent an air of urgency, rather than unreality, to the debates
and made fellowship more meaningful. If war came, it
would come soon. Tambaram might well be the last time
some of these delegations would be able to meet. The very
internationalism of Christianity would, in some cases, single
it out as a dangerous enemy of the State. Only three months
previously Neville Chamberlain had flown back from his
notorious talks with Hitler in Munich at which, in effect,
he handed over Czechoslovakia to the Nazis in payment for
a breathing-space in which Western Europe could press on
with rearmament. Far from guaranteeing peace for a
generation, it hardly procured it for a year.

To no one was this clearer than to Kagawa. The war in
China was still going on. His protests were ineffective and
his pacifism put him out of step with the massive non-
Christian majority of his nation. During the earlier part
of the year he had been busy with new projects. In April
he founded a new Society for the support of his work in
Tokyo. In June he had organized relief for the victims
of a flood which overwhelmed part of Kobe. The month
before he went to Tambaram, he established the *Shinai Hoyo
Noen*, the 'Farm for Health'—an agricultural community
for the rehabilitation of tuberculosis victims—at Teshima,
an island on the inland sea of Setonaikai where he already
had one of his rural projects, including a school and an
orphanage.

He spent a month or two in India, visiting the missions
and churches, addressing meetings and talking with Indian
leaders. As on a previous visit, he had long discussions
with Mahatma Gandhi, the pacifist leader of Indian nationalism. The two men respected each other, though their
views diverged on the subjects of political action and on
the Christian and Hindu bases of service and compassion.

Back in Japan, Kagawa began another society for the support of his work in Osaka, but was distressed that he had to close the 'Farm for Health' less than a year after he had opened it. The Japanese country-folk still maintained their fear of tuberculosis and brought Government pressure to bear on him to have the sufferers removed.

Then, in September 1939, the news he had feared was broadcast to the world. Germany and Russia had invaded Poland. Two days later Britain, and then France, declared war on Germany. In Europe, the lights had gone out once more. Without consulting the national leaders, Lord Linlithgow, Viceroy of India, declared that India, too, was at war with Germany, and Asia was involved with the West in conflict. In his Tokyo home, Kagawa remembered his visit to Europe—the British political leaders he had talked with, the factory workers he had met in Sweden, the co-operative farmers in Norway, the fishermen in Denmark, the hardworking Protestants and Catholics of Holland. He thought of the Indian peasants being recruited from their poverty-stricken villages to fight against aggression, and could not help recalling Mahatma Gandhi's strictures on British imperialism. Even then, he could not picture the future clearly enough to realize that these same peasants, three years later, would be fighting to defend their homeland against the forces of his own nation. Most clearly, he called to mind the Christian friends with whom he had strolled through the lawns of Tambaram.

In the West, the 'cold war' gave place to German advance. The Netherlands were bombed and over-run. Italy entered the war in June 1940 , and shortly afterwards France capitulated and the remnants of the allied armies were evacuated from Dunkirk. The 'Spitfire' pilots of the Royal Air Force prepared to defend Britain against the overwhelming might of the German *Luftwaffe*. In East and

West, the world waited for the news that Hitler had invaded Britain. In Japan, where young men were being recruited at an increasing rate for the war in China, press and radio exulted in the successes of the impregnable Rome-Berlin-Tokyo Axis.

Against a background of rising war hysteria Kagawa the pacifist worked on. Early in 1940 he gained support for a Christian mission to Nanking. A little later he organized relief work after a disastrous fire in Sizuoka city. The tide was beginning to run against the Christian Church, however, and he was soon to feel the strength of it. The Tokyo Students' Consumptive Guild, which he had helped to found, was dissolved. Not a few rejoiced in his loss of face. In the year that followed it became clear that harm rather than good would result from the Western associations of the Church, and the Protestant missionaries began to withdraw. Before the end of 1941, between eight hundred and nine hundred missionaries had reluctantly left Japan, largely through the kindly insistence of their Japanese friends that Government would look more generously on a Church which had no open ties with the West or America.

It was in 1940, when victory seemed securely in the grip of the Axis powers, that Kagawa was arrested for the first time as a traitor. In some American circles he had been respected and almost venerated. The *Helen Topping Calendar* for that year issued a 'Kagawa Number' bearing quotations from his writings and speeches, and in it there was the following message: 'To my brethren in China. Forgive the sin of Japan. Though Japanese Christians have not the power to oppose military force, some of them regret the sin of Japan. I wish the day of reconciliation may soon come.' It was not a message to win sympathy in his own country.

On 25th August he noticed two sullen-looking men

sitting towards the back of the church. They did not rise or kneel as the service proceeded, and the congregation round about them surreptitiously watched with fear in their hearts, praying that their beloved pastor would say nothing to give them offence. They were undoubtedly of the secret police. Kagawa preached, as he so often did in those months, a vigorous sermon on non-violence. As soon as the service was ended the men moved forward, met him at the foot of the pulpit steps and hustled him out through the silent congregation. Almost immediately afterwards it was announced that Pastor Ogawa, a loyal friend of Kagawa, had also been arrested. Both men were taken to the Sugamo prison.

No violence was used against them, and indeed Haru Kagawa was met with respect when she took food for them and was courteously allowed to see her husband. She told him of the protests raised by the Christian community throughout the country, though they both doubted whether such action would be much help in the circumstances. Probably it was not, but Kagawa was not then—or ever, for that matter—without friends in high places. The Foreign Minister, Matsuoka, personally took up his case, intervened with the authorities, and after eighteen days persuaded Katzami, the Minister of Justice himself, to issue an order for his release. He was set free—though only after paying a fine for saying that a labourer was as great as a king!

By September he was preaching again in Osaka before returning to Tokyo. Here he found that, though he might have influential friends, there were plenty of people who regarded him as an enemy. Placards were displayed on the Tokyo hoardings which left him in no doubt of it. 'Death to Kagawa!', they threatened. 'Kagawa is a traitor to Japan!'

Deeply committed as he was to a belief in the power of prayer, he refused to believe that war between Japan and

America was inevitable. It was this, more than the war in Europe, which was uppermost in the minds of the Japanese people. The militarists made no secret of their designs. The conquest of China was a preliminary skirmish, though a long-drawn-out one. It was the prelude to an act of conquest which would make Japan the master of Asia. Axis victories in Europe, though slowed down by Hitler's unaccountable failure to invade Britain, were proof that sudden attack by skilled forces brought victory. The Chinese battlefields were as much training grounds as anything else. Soldiers strutted arrogantly in the towns and young men were sent off proudly by their villages when they were conscripted. The only real hindrance to the plans of the Japanese strategists lay in the armed might of the United States, which had large naval forces centred at Pearl Harbour in the Pacific, and land forces stationed in strength in the Philippines. By comparison, Singapore, held by the British, was completely vulnerable if only Malaya itself could be occupied. With the American forces destroyed or even immobilized Japan could move on to swift victory. About all this there was little doubt either in Tokyo or Washington, though America was reluctant to be drawn into a war which would undoubtedly commit her to action in Europe as well as Asia.

In April 1941, at the invitation of Christians in the United States, a group of eight Japanese, chosen by the National Christian Council of Japan, went to America. At Riverside, California, they spent a fortnight in discussion and prayer with seventeen Americans nominated by the Foreign Missions Conference and the Federal Council of Churches. Their meeting produced a deep and abiding fellowship which was greatly to strengthen the Japanese Church during the years that followed. At the closing session their fellowship was sealed by a solemn covenant of prayer, symbolized by a silver watch-token bearing the inscription, 'Riverside, 1941'. It was also agreed that, as soon as possible, the Americans should make a return visit to Japan.

During his stay in the United States, Kagawa addressed over three hundred meetings in the cause of peace. Not only so, but on his return home he appeared before the Japanese House of Peers to plead for a policy of mediation. The Government listened, but took no action. The militarists were firmly in control.

In November, a highly important development took place in the life of the Japanese Church. Christians were suspect for a number of reasons. They stressed the principle of individual liberty of conscience as against the totalitarianism of Government policy. They believed firmly in democracy. They were linked with the West and America, as the Riverside Conference had proved. Above all, they set loyalty to Christ higher than loyalty to the State or the Emperor. In an attempt to gain more control of the Church, the Government pressed for a union of all Christian Churches. Partly because he believed in co-operating with the Government wherever he could, and partly because he saw unity as guaranteeing greater strength, Kagawa supported the proposal. The *Nippon Kirisuto Kyodan*, a union of Protestant Churches, was formed, and Kagawa became a member of it. He remained loyal to the *Kyodan*, even when other Churches contracted out of it, after the years of war.

At the end of November it was announced that Japanese and American representatives would meet to discuss the possibility of peace between their two countries. On 1st December Kagawa had a telegram to say that American Christians, led by Dr Stanley Jones, would meet too, but in prayer. They would pray, day and night, for peace. Kagawa gathered a group to join them. In Tokyo they began to pray, eating little, pleading for peace. At night

a single candle burned to give them light. At the end of
a week's intercession the candle was blown out. The
diplomatic talks were still going on.

8th December dawned cold and grey in Japan. In the
Kagawa household the family listened to the morning news
broadcast on the radio. There was a break in transmission,
and an order for everyone to wait for important news.
Then came the excited, sibilant voice of the announcer.

'The day of liberation has come at last! Our aircraft have
just completed a surprise attack on the United States Fleet
at Pearl Harbour. The American ships have been destroyed.
Arise, fellow-men of Asia. Japan will lead the way to a
Greater Co-Prosperity sphere in East Asia!'

The Kagawa family sat silent. Outside the quietness was
broken by sirens, hooters and the shrill cries of the crowds.
Sumimoto and his sisters Chiyoko and Umeko stared at
their father. Haru said nothing, looking at the tears on
her husband's stricken face. Toyohiko Kagawa thought of
the candle he had blown out a few hours before. 'I felt',
he wrote afterwards, 'that all the lights of the world had
gone out. My heart was broken.'

Fifty-three years old, half-blind, more stricken by illness
and weakness than he ever allowed anyone to see, he was
to begin a period of anguish such as he had never known
before. As a Christian and a pacifist, he knew he would
be open to attack. He would almost certainly be imprisoned
and perhaps killed. Nothing of that mattered in contrast
with the shame that had come to his nation.

It is not easy either to assess Kagawa's state of mind or
the position he held in the nation during the four years
which followed. Within the Christian community he was
held in high respect as a leader of the *Kyodan*, even though
there were many Christians, misled by the Japanese war-
propaganda of 'liberating Asia', who readily joined the

armed services. It was of course impossible for him to pretend agreement with the national policy. He remained throughout the war a thorough-going pacifist. His pacifism, however, left him as distressed with American militarism as with his own country's, and as the war neared its end, American bombing drew from him uncompromising condemnation. He was out of step with the majority of people in East and West. This brought him into conflict with military leaders and secret police. It did not, however, result in his suffering physical violence. For the greater part of the period he was under surveillance, but his few terms of imprisonment were quite brief. His Christian activity was restricted to preaching, but in this his experience was common to all Christian ministers. What hurt him most, apart from the fact of the war itself, was probably the suspicion and hostility with which he was viewed by ordinary people and his inability to maintain any of his social work. Two facts are worthy of note. The first is that when his war-time activities were scrutinized by the American authorities after they occupied Japan, nothing could be found to suggest that he had in any way supported the war effort, much less encouraged an anti-American spirit. The other is that, despite this, before the war ended he was once more called in by the Government to assist and advise in their welfare programmes for war-sufferers. There were, in fact, not a few in authority who continued to have a high regard for him even though they found it hard to tolerate his disloyalty to the national cause.

For a short time after the outbreak of war he sought refuge at his rural settlement at Teshima, on the Inland Sea, in order to try and come to terms with the new situation. The respite was brief, for the settlement was closed down by Government order and the navy took over the great lake for the testing of submarine equipment. It was the first of many limitations put on him. He had by this time written over one hundred and thirty books, but he quickly saw that booksellers were no longer displaying them. No writer had been more popular throughout the country. Queues had often formed outside the booksellers on the morning of the publication of a new novel or a book of poems; late-comers might be disappointed, for the first printings were often sold out astonishingly quickly. Now, all his books were withdrawn from sale. Many were publicly burned. He could not find a publisher who would accept a new manuscript. Indeed, the only books available to the public were some volumes of his prose poems.

On the other hand, at this point there was little restriction placed on his evangelistic work. A Christian village settlement had been established in Manchuria, and in August 1942 he was permitted to go and spend a month there holding an evangelical campaign. The mental strain of the past months and the vigour of the campaign left him prostrate. When he returned to Japan he fell seriously ill with pneumonia, and spent four weeks in the Nakano Medical Guild Hospital, going afterwards to Kobe to recuperate. Not until December was he fit to take up his normal work once more.

The months passed. He moved about the country, speaking and preaching. Just as, in earlier days, he had found it impossible to preach about the Cross without mentioning food, now he found it impossible not to plead for international goodwill and to denounce war. After addressing a huge meeting in Kobe in May 1943 he was arrested by the secret police and charged with being a pacifist and a socialist. It was difficult to make much capital out of such a charge, and after a short period of detention he was released.

Meanwhile Japan moved from success to success. It was

to take a long time for the United States to recover from her losses at Pearl Harbour, and in Asia and the Middle East Britain was being hard pressed. Malaya was successfully invaded. Japanese warships attacked the island fortress of Singapore, which was quickly captured by troops from the mainland. Indonesia and the Philippines, bastions of Dutch and American strength, fell before the apparently invincible Japanese forces, followed by Burma and much of New Guinea. India itself was threatened, and it seemed as if nothing could hold back the surging tide of victory. More and more of Asia was 'liberated'. In Japan itself, everything was increasingly geared to the war effort. Men up to sixty and women up to forty were conscripted for munition work. Students were often expected to work for six days a week in the war effort, leaving only one for study. Decorative banners hung outside the homes of recruits to the three services, and villages held proud gatherings to send their men to war.

The increasing tempo of war-propaganda brought still sterner condemnation from Kagawa. Wherever he went he was shadowed and whatever he said was taken down and reported to headquarters. In November, six months after his arrest at Kobe, he was once more taken by the secret police, this time in Tokyo. On this occasion he was questioned, almost without cessation, for nine days and nights before he was released. It was evident that the Intelligence Department was convinced that he was engaged in spying activities for the Americans. At the same time, messages in his name were being broadcast to the United States urging American Christians not to fight against their Japanese Christian brethren. He had as little to do with the one as the other. As a result of the Tokyo arrest, however, he was forbidden to engage in any activity except preaching, and that only in his own church. His schools had been shut. His orphanages were turned into depots for the war-effort. His rural and town settlements were all closed down. The anti-Christian movement of the Government was well under way.

Despite this, twice during 1944, in April and October, he was permitted to go to China. The first time was in April, as a member of the Committee for a second experimental village settlement in Manchuria; the second, beginning in October, was an evangelistic preaching-tour. On the second occasion he spent four months in China, strengthening the Chinese Christians by his fellowship, but for his own part appalled at the growing strength of Communism underground.

In Japan, the radio and the press recorded victory after victory. The common people, long conditioned to accept what they were told, had no doubt that Japan was master of nearly all Asia and the Americans almost completely defeated. The cost of victory was nevertheless becoming more apparent. Little white boxes, containing the ashes of heroes who had died in the service of their country, came back in larger numbers. There were more flags outside the town homes of those whose sons or fathers had died in action. In the country, white posts, four feet high, served the same purpose outside village homes. The stoicism of the Buddhist and the national pride of the Shintoist forbade people to question whether the cost was worth paying. By the end of 1944, however, not even the carefully edited accounts of the war in the West could disguise the fact that Britain and America, with the immense power of Russia thrown on to their side, were moving towards victory in Europe. The very name of Russia was still enough to anger the old Japanese.

As the war went on, Kagawa's personal position became more obscure both in Japan and in America. It was in a sense a compliment to his greatness that both the warring powers should claim him as they did. His name was used by both sides in their 'war of nerves' and in their publicity broadcasts, so that Christians in Japan and outside of it were left wondering if he were really in the pay of 'the other side'. From Kagawa's own point of view, the worst instance of this was a 'psychological' broadcast from America, when the American authorities asserted that after Japan's defeat he was to become the ruler of Japan, under United States guidance. It was intended to leave the Japanese people in no doubt about American victory and about their pacific intentions once the war was over.

Kagawa himself, who heard the broadcast, was astounded. Certainly no such suggestion had ever been made to him, but it put him in a more unhappy position with the Japanese than he had been before, for the militarists were able, with good reason, to denounce him as a traitor and gain the support of the common people for their claim. Kagawa, in his turn, broadcast to the Japanese nation an assurance that the American story was completely false and that he remained a loyal citizen of his own country. Kagawa's broadcast, in its turn, was monitored to the United States. Naturally, it contained no reference to his continued pacifism, for it would have been contrary to the Government's policy to allow such a statement. The result was that, in Japan, the stigma of his possible betrayal remained in many minds which could not entirely forget the American broadcasts, while in the United States and amongst their allies, the broadcast was construed to mean that he had given up his pacifism and allied himself with the Japanese war-effort.

To those who implicitly believed what they were told, that Japan was still driving the Americans before them, the first United States air attacks on the Japanese islands came as a frightening shock. Kagawa, who had never ceased to oppose his own Government, now openly denounced the Americans. By the beginning of 1945, war casualties were coming back in larger numbers and it was impossible to deceive the more alert minds. Even if Japan was not being beaten, she was having to fight hard to hold her own. It was at this time that the Government once more turned to Kagawa, as it had done in the days of the Tokyo earthquake. Possibly those in power felt they would be wise to have him on their side, if possible, in case the worst happened. At any rate, in March 1945 he was appointed Chairman of the Government's War-time Relief Committee.

Possibly because of this very fact, he received threats of assassination, and a story was circulated that he had gone into hiding in the forest near Tokyo. In fact, by June, just after the surrender of Germany and the suicide of Hitler in Berlin, he was appointed Adviser to the Welfare Ministry, whose main care was for the war sufferers and in particular those whose homes had been destroyed by bombing. It was a work very close to his heart. Unable to do anything about his settlement work, he found here an outlet for his compassion. Bearing the cross, as he had done through the years of war, he found a relief of spirit in sharing the sufferings of others once more. The impression, given in some accounts, that he suddenly emerged from four years of obscurity when the Americans occupied Japan is far from the truth. He had been a force to be reckoned with, both within and outside the Church, right through the war, and was beginning to take his place in public life again before it ended.

In July, in spite of the official assurances that all was going well, the Japanese Government knew that they were going to lose the war, though they envisaged a long and bitter struggle before it ended. In that month Kagawa broadcast a personal message to America: 'Americans, return to the spirit of Abraham Lincoln!' It was a passionate plea that the United States forces should show true humanity in their time of conquest. A month later, to the horror of the whole world, the first atom bombs were dropped on Hiroshima and Nagasaki. In the latter, every patient, nurse and doctor, every first and second year student, and all but four of the medical faculty of the university, were killed. Japan, whose fatalistic inhabitants had faced flood, famine, fire and earthquake with stoical calm, was stricken beyond description. The Emperor's broadcast on 15th August fell on the ears of a nation which had been cast down from dreams of world conquest to the depths of despair.

'I have ordered all hostilities to cease.'

The war was over; Japan was defeated. There seemed nothing left to live for, and even the dead had died in vain.

CHAPTER ELEVEN

The Problems of Peace

S HOCKED by the tragedies of Hiroshima and Nagasaki,
and still almost incredulous of the fact that they had
been defeated when, even during the American bombing
of Japan, their Government had assured them that they
were really winning the war, the Japanese people were
assailed by a new terror. Propaganda had conditioned them
into believing that the Americans were a savage, violent
and lustful army who had perpetrated indescribable atrocities on the prisoners they had captured. It is a familiar phase
in war-making, and is seldom confined to one side. Now,
with the Emperor's words of surrender in their ears, they
waited the coming of the victors. They expected no mercy
from their terrible enemies.

On 25th August the American soldiers arrived in their
transports and began to disembark in Tokyo. They wore
full war-kit, talked in loud voices and seemed to tower
above the small-made inhabitants of the city. The contrast
of the next few hours and days with the horrors they had
expected was almost too much for the stricken Japanese.
Instead of lust they found kindness; instead of cruelty they
saw compassion. True, the soldiers had little idea of the
magnitude of the problems of peace-making, but they took
chocolate, candy and unwanted rations from their packs
and doled them out to the children who soon began to
run after them. As they watched them snatching from each
other, greedily eating what they could get hold of, the

soldiers began to realize that they had come to a hungry land. They noticed the thin bodies. The burnt-out sectors of the blitzed city were all too obvious. Bitter though they were about the war, hating the Japanese against whom they had fought, the essential sentimentality of the American soldier soon became the most noticeable quality of the victors who poured into the city. They found themselves sorry for the enemy they had conquered. Before long, the Japanese began to respond to their advances. The first fears of reprisal gave place to new hope.

Above the Atsugi airport the sun shone on a silver aeroplane, landing smoothly on the airstrip. From it stepped General Douglas MacArthur, Supreme Commander of the Allied Forces in the Pacific. As he moved on to Japanese soil, the line of Government officials who waited to greet him knew that the end of the war had really come. The tall, distinguished soldier was the living symbol that Japan was in enemy hands. The occupation of the country had begun.

The Japanese capitulation was extraordinarily complete. The atom-bombs seemed not merely to have blasted cities into nothingness; they had also destroyed the militarist legend of invincibility. With it had gone much else—any hope of saving themselves, even an ability to think for themselves. Almost at once it seemed clear to MacArthur that he had the opportunity, with the ready co-operation of the nation's leaders, to build a new country, a democratized Japan. The Communist element had not had time to make itself felt. The nation, having suffered complete loss of 'face', was prepared to obey its conquerors.

Through the period of Kagawa's life the Japanese ability to come to terms with disaster or adversity and begin again had been constantly demonstrated. No nation learns more quickly than Japan, or puts to use more effectively the lessons it learns. No country has been more swift to take up materials it had previously discarded when it has realized that they were likely to be useful. So it was now, immediately after the war. Autocracy and dictatorship had been discredited. Democracy must be the new pattern of successful living.

The great Japanese exponent of democracy, selflessness and service had been Dr Kagawa. Discarded and despised as his ideas had been during the advance in Asia, national leaders now saw him as the most typical, and indeed the most distinguished, example of the way they wished to go. It was because of this, rather than because he was a Christian, that they turned to him in the post-war period. He had already been brought back to a position of responsibility before the war ended. Now, from every side, came appeals for his help.

The first appeal was from the Prime Minister himself, though here, at least, there was more than a desire to be led into the safe road of democracy. Messengers came from Prince Higashi-Kuni, the Premier, seeking Kagawa at his little house. He was not there, but had gone away to think in the forests beyond Tokyo. When he returned home and learned of the messages from the Prince he was at first reluctant to respond to them. He foresaw a recall to public life and wished to avoid it. Then, at last, when a third official came, he gave way and went to meet the Prime Minister in his office.

'Dr Kagawa,' said the Prince, 'Japan has been destroyed, not because we had not a sufficient army, but because we had suffered the loss of a good standard of morality and engaged in war. We need a new standard of ethics, like that of Jesus Christ. Buddhism can never teach us to forgive our enemies; nor can Shintoism. Only Jesus Christ was able to love his enemies. Therefore, Dr Kagawa, if

Japan is to be revived we need Jesus Christ as the basis of our national life. I want you to help me to put the love of Jesus Christ into the hearts of our people.'

The Christian leader was deeply moved. He promised to serve in any way possible—except by taking office in the Government. One of his first requests when the Prime Minister asked how his own desire could be made effective was that all Christian preachers and ministers in prison should at once be released. He needed assistance, too, to set going certain social ventures.

Kagawa's dearest schemes had suffered greatly. The Labour Unions had been dissolved by military decree. The Co-operative Movement which he had helped to found, numbering seven million members, had been put under Government direction. The National Anti-war Movement had, naturally, been disbanded. His rural reconstruction schemes had been abandoned. The Settlement houses in Tokyo, Osaka and Kobe had been bombed by the Americans and destroyed. These, however, could not immediately be dealt with. Japan was not only defeated; its people were almost starving. Tens of thousands of refugees were homeless. The situation of twenty years earlier, when Tokyo had been almost decimated by the earthquake, was now repeated throughout the country. This was the really desperate problem, as urgent as preaching itself. To share in it was to help to carry the Cross; to put the love of Jesus, as the Prince had asked, into the hearts of the people.

At the beginning of September Kagawa wrote 'An Open Letter to General MacArthur' in the *Yoriuma* newspaper of Japan urging the treatment of the fallen enemy in Christian love. Shortly afterwards, at the General's request, he went to see him to discuss how this might be put into practice. Kagawa's first suggestion was as practical as ever. He drew the General's attention to the homeless and hungry refugees who crowded the streets of the capital, pointed out the virtual certainty that instead of supporting democracy they would turn to Communism unless something were done at once, and asked that food shops should be opened and rations released from American stores. Characteristically, he also insisted that strict measures should be taken to prevent food getting into wrong hands and a 'black market' being allowed to operate because of American generosity.

Within a month after the capitulation, Kagawa was already beginning again to be a public figure. He refused to allow himself to be considered as a member of the Cabinet, though the Prime Minister wished him to do so. Instead, he extended his activities of the previous few months and became Adviser to the Department of Public Welfare. The American authorities had no wish to govern Japan, only to help it to govern itself in a democratic fashion. The normal agencies of Government, reconstituted, restaffed and redirected, continued to function. In addition, city life had to begin all over again and many national societies for the benefit of the country were begun. Kagawa found himself involved at every level of this national reconstruction. Before October was past he had become Welfare Adviser to Kobe City (which allowed him to give attention to his own settlement work there), managing director of the National Nutrition Society, and a member of the Committee set up by Government to discuss the inauguration of a new parliamentary system and the holding of elections.

One of the most moving events of these months was the arrival of a group of American Church leaders in Japan. They were the very same men who had met at Riverside the year the war began, and it was the first time they had

had an opportunity of fulfilling their promise to meet the Japanese Church. During the war they had prayed together, across the vast reaches of the Pacific Ocean, and the sense of this fellowship across the frontiers was one of the facts that had helped to sustain Kagawa during the darkest days of the war. The delegation found their friend older, thinner, but unshaken in faith. 'Dr Kagawa', they wrote, 'has lost a quarter of his weight, but is still the same fine Christian leader.' Despite the many claims on his time, the Church came first in his life, and he found many opportunities to meet with his American friends in conference, worship and prayer. His spirit was exemplified in a prayer he offered at the close of one of the first meetings they had together.

'O God,' he prayed, 'we thank Thee that the war is over, that the clouds have parted and the sun shines again. Bless the Christians of China, Korea, the United States and all the world, and build Thy Church, O God, not out of stone, brick or wood, which may be destroyed, but out of living souls made strong in Thy spirit. Amen.'

For two months the delegation remained in Japan, surprised at the friendliness of their reception and the determination of the nation to remake its policy on a Christian conception of democracy. Before they left the country they had time to see how busy Kagawa himself was going to be in shaping the future.

In November the Japanese Socialist party was re-established, with Kagawa as a leading figure. A fortnight later there was a meeting to inaugurate the Japanese Co-operative Union. Kagawa became its president. At the beginning of December he was elected President of the Japanese Teachers' Union. In February 1946 he was made a member of the Food Production Committtee of the Government, and two months later he established the Christian Newspaper Press. His books began to appear once more in the shops and on the bookstalls. In June he promoted the New Japan Building Movement and in August was made a member of the Council of the World Movement for Federal Government. A little later he became President of the National Farmers' Union. It was an astonishing range of activities for a Christian minister of almost sixty, who was constantly on the brink of ill-health and for four years had been commonly regarded as a traitor to his country. Yet, if he had wished, he could have had much greater honour.

When elections were held in the early part of 1946 he was urged by his friends to stand as a candidate for Parliament. The authorities would have avoided the indignity of anyone even voting against him and offered him a seat in the House of Peers. His answer both to his friends and officialdom was the same. 'I cannot do this. I must give my time to preaching. My father was a politician, but in my youth I promised God that I would preach the story of the Cross. I can listen only to His inner voice.'

The elections took place. Kagawa would undoubtedly have found a seat in the House of Representatives even if he had not wished to sit in the House of Peers. Instead, he did as he had said. He gave his time primarily not to the organizations of which he was a member but to the preaching of the Gospel. Alongside the swing to democracy went a new interest in Christianity. Kagawa's services were crowded, and always inquirers came to talk with him further about Christ and His Cross. 'To worship with him was to live in a larger world', wrote one visitor. 'To share in the Sacrament of Holy Communion as he conducted it was to be transported to the Upper Room itself.' The preaching of the Cross was essential to the resurrection of the land he loved.

Chaos in all the world;
In Japan
Defeat. . . .
Poverty. . . .
Utter destitution. . . .
Yet there is also love
That gives and shares,
Thankfulness,
Sacrifice,
And silent uncomplaint.

For where the Spirit of the Cross
Shines deep
Within their hearts,
God's saints
Await the Day of Glory
And His Kingdom
Has already come.

The Kingdom
Has already come
To this world
Through the Cross;
And Christ's disciples
Living in His life
    Bring Light.

Light even to
The shacks destroyed by war;
And to the land laid low
By storm and earthquake.
So to him who cries,
'Japan is ruined!' I would say,
'You must forget your Self,
And you must learn to love.'

For lo,
The Kingdom is
Not here, nor there;
The Kingdom is
Within the soul,
Not to be seen,
But felt.

Yes, verily, I know
That only through the Kingdom
There will some day come
The resurrection of Japan.

It was in 1946, about the time of the election of the new Parliament, that Emperor Hiro-hito showed his own greatness. He had traditionally been regarded as a demi-god, accepting the worship of his people as the right of one who was the descendant of the Sun-Goddess. When he had announced the surrender of Japan he had taken upon himself the blame for the war. Now he went farther. He declared that he was in no sense divine, that he did not desire the worship of his subjects, that he was an ordinary man. He came out to mix with his people, to share their sorrows and help to lead them in their new life. But he, like all his people, needed direction.

A few months after this announcement, an official appeared at the Kagawa household with a letter bearing the Imperial seal. The Emperor wished to see Dr Kagawa, that he might learn something of the Christian way. Some men might have regarded such a summons as the crowning achievement of their life. It drove the humble leader to his knees. He had only half an hour in which to explain to the Emperor the meaning of the Cross. How could such a thing be done? In fact, it was not done—or not in half an hour.

The Imperial Palace had been bombed and was unusable. Kagawa made his way to the offices not far away which were being used instead. Here he was conducted to the presence of the Emperor, and bowed ceremoniously before the short, dark man with the keen, intelligent face. The Emperor sat down. Kagawa stood in front of him, and began to speak. The exposition went on, and the fingers of the clock moved past the half-hour and even the hour. The Emperor listened, asked questions, but did not even look at his watch. Outside the door of his room the palace officials were flustered and uneasy. The talk within the room continued. Not until an hour and three-quarters were over did the Emperor give a hint that the interview must end. Then Kagawa drew from his robe a tattered copy of the Bible, the very book that had sustained him through the bitter years of the war. He opened it and began to read.

'Whosoever would be great amongst you must be the servant of all.' He went on to say that only through service can a man or a nation be great. Then, watched by the astonished officials, he left the palace and went home, a preacher who saw no difference between the need of kings and the need of common people.

CHAPTER TWELVE

A Sort of Retirement

ON 28TH APRIL 1952 Japan moved into a new era. On that date the Peace Treaty was signed, seven years after the war had ended, and the American 'Occupation' came to an end. Politically, the country was more stable than might have been expected. Neither the old conservative die-hards, the pre-war directors of policy, nor the Communists who had used the depression after the war for their own ends, dominated the Government. The Emperor, shorn of his mythical status, had gained new stature as a human being. The personal devotion of his subjects to him, in spite of his attempt to take the responsibility for the war on his shoulders and so relieve the militarist clique who were its real perpetrators, prevented the rise of pressure-groups and dictatorships seen in so many other countries. Economically, because of the Japanese people's resilience and their readiness to work extremely hard without asking for immediate luxury or increased relaxation as the price of their labour, the country began to leap forward once more. In Japan, as in Western Germany, there was a desire to put the memory of the war behind and make up for the lost years. There was, too, a very real resolve to regain the respect of the world, and prosperity as much as penance seemed the way to this end. Internationally, Japan was once more recognized as a sovereign State, and this was all the more easy because she showed no intention of grasping again the 'great power' status which, in any case, in Asia had passed to China and India. On 18th December 1956 Japan was admitted as the eightieth member of the United Nations. By that time she had diplomatic ties with seventy-one nations, and was officially represented in almost every independent State in the world.

What of religion in Japan during these years? More especially, what had happened to the Christian Church since the war?

In 1945 one of the first Governmental acts had been to separate religion from State-control. All religions were given complete freedom to worship and to preach. Shinto ceased to be the State religion. The Emperor no longer demanded the worship of his loyal subjects. The immediate result was not so much a strengthening of the traditional religions as a swift mushrooming of strange sects. In 1945, when the enactment of religious liberty was promulgated, there were forty-five religious 'denominations'. By 1950, there were almost twenty times that number, somewhere between seven hundred and fifty and eight hundred. Some of these were doubtless perfectly sincere attempts to find a satisfying kind of faith. More were the result of small groups of disciples gathering round religious eccentrics. The greater number were very probably the result of the fact that religious 'leaders' were exempt from many national duties, and perhaps more important, that their places of worship were free from tax. It is not surprising that private houses were turned into 'temples' and notice-boards advertising the 'Culture Denomination', the 'Thunder God Denomination' or the 'Righteousness Sightseeing Association' appeared outside ordinary dwelling-houses. If there was insufficient room inside these wooden homes for many worshippers, that did not matter. The adherents of many of these extraordinary sects were mostly very few. The importance, at a deeper level, of this religiosity was that it showed that the Japanese people had lost faith in much that their ancestors had held sacred, and yet felt the need to worship. Post-war Japan was an example of a people who *must* worship, and yet were unsure of what or whom they ought to worship.

Within the Christian community, Protestants and Roman Catholics had both gained ground. In the twenty-five years since Kagawa had begun the 'Kingdom of God Movement', the Roman Catholic Church had increased its membership by more than fifty per cent, though Protestantism had grown by only about ten per cent. The Orthodox Church, on the other hand, had lost some seventy-five per cent of its membership.

The *Kyodan*, the 'United Church', remained the main grouping of Protestant denominations. This surprised some of its critics. It was not a 'United Church' in the sense of the Church of South India. Rather, it was a federation of denominations, not difficult to join and easy to leave. Some did leave. Not all the Anglicans had even been within it, and those who had joined seceded after the war. So did the Lutherans. So did some, but not all, of the Baptists and the Presbyterians. Reasons varied, from theology to the need of maintaining financial support from overseas. The removal of major denominations with international links weakened the Union but did not disrupt or destroy it. The *Kyodan* remained the principal Christian federation in Japan, claiming more than sixty per cent of Japanese Protestants amongst its membership.

Where did Kagawa fit into this political and ecclesiastical background? Is it possible to come to an accurate assessment of his significance in the life of Japan?

He had never desired to be a public figure, though his literary and social work made him one, and his relentless pacifism gained him a notoriety which was just as nation-wide.

His re-emerging into public life during the closing months of the war and the years following it was not of his own desiring. He was, however, one of the few really mature figures of Japan, free from self-seeking and trusted by both sides. Bernard Rubens in the United States army periodical, *Pacific Stars and Stripes*, had accused him of anti-American activities during the war, and it was well known that he had condemned the American bombing of Japanese cities. But then, he had equally condemned militarism and atrocities amongst his own people. Professor Richard T. Baker, sent from Columbia University to investigate the behaviour of Christian leaders during the war, completely exonerated him in his book, *Darkness of the Sun*. The Tokyo Christian Council and the *Kyodan* spoke strongly in his defence. As a result, he was able to gain the confidence of General MacArthur and speak effectively about the needs of his people.

From the point of view of the Japanese Government it would have been stupid to have overlooked him. He had had tremendous experience in welfare projects, he had worked closely with high-ranking members of Government and the Civil Service, and the swing from Conservatism to Socialism made it natural for him to be consulted in the many co-operative schemes which were put in hand and in which he had been a highly-criticized pioneer in pre-war years. He was ready to serve on newly-constituted 'boards', to act as director or adviser. When he was urged to become a member of the House of Peers he saw the honour clearly enough, both to himself and the Church. But his refusal was quite definite.

Why did he refuse? In the answer to this question are implicit some of the essentials to an assessment of his character. It was partly because he shied away from the identification of Christianity with any political party. Partly, too, because he was an individualist—a fact which had been evident throughout his ministry. Most of all, it was because he regarded his main work, particularly after the war, as 'evangelism'.

Not the least relevant reason, however, was that he was an elderly and sick man. No one would have realized it had they only heard of his activities between, say, 1945 and 1948, for few people were busier, but those who worked alongside him saw it and waited for the inevitable breakdown. He was gravely underweight. Trachoma, the eye-disease that had robbed him of one eye and impaired the other, often gave him intense pain. His lungs constantly gave him trouble, and he found breathing difficult. The breakdown came, and in 1948 he collapsed. His close friends and his family wondered if, this time, he could pull through. After an illness lasting three months he began to recover once more. This time, however, even Kagawa himself agreed that he must go slow. His more active life was over. He must accept some sort of retirement.

It was a remarkably inadequate word to describe the years that followed. He continued to speak, to dictate, to travel and to advise. In 1950 he set out on a world tour which he spent largely in the United States and Britain. He fulfilled endless speaking engagements on these visits, and though his voice was weaker, there was a luminosity about him which made him seem like a man apart. Those who spoke and wrote of him at this time compared him with Dr Schweitzer and St Francis of Assisi. Others spoke of him as the Gandhi of Japan. No comparison really fitted him. Like all truly great world figures, he was in some ways different from everyone else. But that the Christ he loved dwelt in him, that the Light of the World glowed through all he said and did, there could be no doubt.

This he intended to be his last venture out of the East.

Four years later, nonetheless, he went to the Assembly of the World Council of Churches at Evanston as a 'consultant' representative of the National Christian Council of Japan.

Kagawa has never been without critics, either inside or outside the Church. Not even his Christian faith and experience rendered him immune from them, and indeed the strength of his convictions on some points resulted in the criticism being even more pointed. It has been said that, particularly amongst some Americans, he has been lauded unreasonably as a super-man. Every great man suffers as much from the adulation of his friends as from the attacks of his enemies, and it would be quite false to imply that he is the only great modern Japanese Christian. At the same time, he was undoubtedly the pioneer in Christian social work of any magnitude. His status as a writer may wane, but it is undeniable that few writers of his time, especially in the world of non-fiction, had such a large reading public or were so prolific in their output. Something like a hundred and fifty books published in fifty years would be no small achievement for a professional writer who gave his time to nothing else. He was dismissed, when the 'World Church' conception gathered momentum, as being on the side-lines of the ecumenical movement. In one sense this was undoubtedly true. He had little patience with 'denominationalism', especially when it implied the offering to non-Christian lands by diverse missionary societies of a 'broken' instead of a 'united' Body of Christ. On the other hand, he cut across denominational boundaries, gave Christians a feeling of belonging to each other, and stood by the *Kyodan* which, however it began, is undoubtedly an ecumenical movement. He recognized the historical differences which lay behind a divided Christendom, but was impatient with those who spent over-much time debating the theology of Church, ministry and sacraments when, as he saw it, the task of the Church was to proclaim one Lord and one Gospel. Not least, he was criticized by narrow, literalist Christians as not being 'Bible-centred' in his preaching. Yet no other Japanese preacher of his time drew such great crowds at his evangelistic meetings.

Perhaps the most useful way of summarizing his contribution to the stock of contemporary Japanese Christianity is to watch him at work during these years of 'retirement'.

He plunged into the slums in 1909, because he wanted to offer Christ to the degraded inhabitants of Shinkawa. It was as a preacher that he met his gracious, staunch wife and helper, Haru Shiba. He refused to take an official position in the days of Tokyo 'reconstruction' because he wanted two days out of every three for evangelism. When he went to China, it was not as a Christian ambassador presenting the better side of Japanese nature, but as a preacher. 'The Kingdom of God Movement' was straightforward evangelism. In the war, though he had seen his settlement work destroyed, the real deprivation, which he never completely suffered, would have come if he had been forbidden to preach. In the years of his retirement it was evangelism that took up most of his time.

In Tokyo, of course, he had his own church. Fortunately neither the church nor his home had been destroyed in the American raids; nor had the school or the orphanage. Once the war was over the Kagawa house became the centre of immense activity again. Whenever a visitor arrived at the house, he would see a line of Western shoes and home-made *geta*, the thick wooden-soled sandals, outside the front door. Always, it seemed, the *Sensei* was overwhelmed with visitors. As one went, another came. The study, with its Western-type chairs and its round table piled with books and papers, was crowded, and in the hum of voices it was difficult to hear what any one person was saying. In the centre of all the activity, the slim, elderly man with the eager gestures and the gentle voice answered questions, gave advice, or talked to his church staff or his secretary. When the three children were younger, he and his wife had taken them every night to the church, to sleep in the vestry, so that they might have some relief from the constant bustle of their home. Now they were older, the children had dispersed. Umeko, the daughter, was in America, finishing her studies before moving on to serve in the World Council of Churches—a fitting gift from Japan to the ecumenical movement. From the subdued busyness of the house, Kagawa would move out to take services in the church. Here he was most truly himself. The endless conversation of the household died away. The claims of those who needed help were, for the moment, put on one side.

The church is a simple one, with a single bell in the steeple. There are no pews, only chairs. There is no chancel, no robed choir, only a pulpit and a small reed-organ. The student who, at the age of twenty, inveighed against those who worship churches rather than God had become the minister who would have nothing in his church-building which would distract the worshippers' attention from God. The congregation packs in, doctors, apprentices, housewives, labourers, government servants, old men and women bent with age, and boys and girls who find it hard to sit still. There are so many who want to find room that those who come late must sit on the floor in front. They come not because the preacher is a famous man, but because he has something important to say. And they know that, somewhere in his words, his reading, his prayers, there will be the theme of the Cross and God's redeeming love.

For a considerable part of each year, however, Kagawa

had to leave his colleagues in charge of the church and his secretaries in command of his office. These were the months when he was on tour, conducting evangelistic missions throughout the country. From Hokkaido in the far north to Kyushu in the extreme south he preached the same theme as he did in his home church. Often these tours were undertaken alone. But he was never more content than when he shared them with one or other of his American friends. One of these was Dr William Axling, his first biographer, who gave fifty years of his missionary service to Japan. Another was his most intimate friend, Dr Stanley Jones, whom he had often met and with whom he shared a week's vigil of prayer in the days before the attack on Pearl Harbour.

Only Stanley Jones could command crowds anything like as large as those who came to hear Kagawa. Five times they toured the country together. Halls and churches were packed to capacity. But whether alone or in a preaching team, Kagawa never spoke without effect. Not only scores, but often hundreds of listeners signed forms of dedication or inquiry. It is true that not all those who did so were gathered into the Church. If that was not the preacher's failure, since the responsibility was left in the hands of the local church, neither was it always the fault of the church itself; for lack of money in the post-war years made it impossible to staff churches adequately, and not infrequently pastors had to undertake some other work in order to support their families. The fact remains that in Japan, as much as in any other country in Asia, there are thousands of unchurched folk who have a deep love of the Christ whom Kagawa proclaimed.

Just as he maintained his evangelistic approach, so he never wavered from his pacifist position. It had got him into trouble in school and college, alienated him from many of his supporters in the labour movement, and singled him out as an enemy of the State during the war. His most characteristic appearance in this field occurred in 1954. In that year he had been elected a vice-president of the World Movement for Federal Government. But that year, too, something happened which shocked the whole world. Twenty-three Japanese fishermen became the centre of international attention. They were infected, with tragic results, by the atomic fall-out from an experimental nuclear explosion at Bikini atoll. Two men, widely known in the world Church for their quite different contributions to it, addressed a packed, emotional meeting in Tokyo. They were Kagawa and Dr Emil Brunner, the famous German theologian. Without reserve, they denounced war and pleaded for international control of atomic energy.

There are plenty of people who regard writing as a means of filling in time or making money. To Kagawa, who used all he earned for the compassionate schemes he supported, it was a vocation. Few of his books have achieved fame outside Japan, though there first printings were frequently sold out before the date of publication. Many of his books were pointed towards the contemporary situation and became out of date with the passage of time. Others dealt with psychology, sociology or economics, and had a limited public. His novels will be read, if they are read at all, for their 'period' interest, because the world they reflect is largely gone. Some of his books, notably his meditations, devotional commentaries and more particularly his poems, continue to circulate in many countries. A writer's influence is not to be judged, however, merely by the number of his reprints or even of his readers. Though Kagawa's writings may be forgotten, except for some of the more moving poems or paragraphs, they had immense importance in their day, as two examples will readily show.

The first is, of course, the publication in book form of
Across the Death-line. With this novel he leapt into the front
rank of Japanese writers, scoring a best-selling success.
What was of far greater importance was the fact that the
novel helped to change the face of Japan's industrial cities,
drawing attention as it did to the degradation of the slums.

A second, less widely known story comes from Indonesia. In Sumatra one of the miracles of modern Christianity is the emergence of the Batak Church and its
steadfastness under Japanese occupation. The Rev. Wishar
Saragih was the first ordained minister to come from the
Simelungen section of this Church. During the occupation
he came across one of Kagawa's books dealing with rural
evangelism, containing stories of his work amongst Japanese
peasants and his training of laymen to be evangelists to
their own people. Saragih felt that this was precisely what
was needed in his own island. Basing his work on the
example of a man he had never met, a fellow-countryman
of the soldiers who had conquered Sumatra, by the end of
two years Saragih had more than a thousand men who had
offered themselves as 'witnesses' for the areas beyond the
great lake which separated the Batak Church from the non-
Christian tribes. Coming for instruction once a month,
they were sent out at the end of a year as a new and im-
pressive force of evangelists. A writer who can stir a
young Church to new ventures of faith, in a land where
he was not known, cannot be dismissed as of negligible
importance.

In 1954, the *Kyodan* showed a new awareness of its really
being a united Church of Christ. It produced a Confession
of Faith which gained general assent. It instituted a Board
of Foreign Missions, as well as pledging itself to full co-
operation with and support of other Protestant Churches.
It planned for a new evangelistic 'arm', which would train

teams of lay and ministerial evangelists for work in town and country. Kagawa's influence can be seen especially in the last project.

It was seen just as clearly in the activities of the National Christian Council of Japan at this same period. Typhoons and floods struck at the towns of Kyushu, Tohoku and Hokkaido and the Joban area. Fires ravaged Noshiro and Odate cities. Japan had long been accustomed to these calamities. For centuries they had been accepted with Buddhist stoicism, if not with indifference. They were not only part of life, but the out-working of fate itself. Now times had changed. Blankets, food, clothing and medicine were rushed to the distressed areas where the Church shared with the Government in the work of relief. Not a few who heard of these things remembered that it was Kagawa, as much as any other single person, who had planned relief schemes in Tokyo and Yokohama after the 1923 earthquake and pioneered in the very services which the nation now took for granted.

The 'Occupation' had resulted in an increase of prostitution and a shattering rise in the number of illegitimate children. Settlement homes for street girls rescued from their profession, orphanages for unwanted children, sanatoria for tuberculosis patients who had become more numerous owing to the privations of the war years, as well as hostels for working-men, were also set up under the guidance of the National Christian Council. Here, too, the pattern went back to Kagawa, though because of his interest in this kind of work many others had taken it up and studied it in other countries.

It is impossible to separate two other aspects of the National Christian Council's work at this time from Kagawa's influence, much though they owed in detail to innumerable other people. The first is Japan World Church Service.

Closely linked with schemes inaugurated by the World Council of Churches and supported by the generosity of the United States, emergency relief was provided for refugees (especially those from Korea during the war), for inadequately paid ministers, and for many others in need. It is easy to see how close to Kagawa's own heart were such schemes as the importation of chicks for the stocking of poor Japanese farms, the provision of clover seeds for the pioneer farm area of Tohoku, the establishment of 'good-will industries' for the handicapped and mentally defective, and the gift of vitamin tablets for pastors' families. These were the very things for which he had pleaded in articles, books and pamphlets dealing with the needs of rural areas.

The second of the National Christian Council schemes in which he was closely involved again concerned the countryside. The Christian Council set up a special department of Rural Evangelism. If Kagawa was interested in providing poor farmers with clover seeds and chicks, he was far more concerned to offer them the Christian Gospel. A Farmers' Gospel School was established at the Council's Rural Institute, based on those which Kagawa had run at such places as Teshima before the war. A Rural Welfare Research Institute was set up at Mitaka, at the Christian University near Tokyo. In April 1953 a popular Christian magazine for farmers, *Noson*, began publication. It seemed almost inevitable that Kagawa should become its editor-in-chief. The whole aim of these projects was to take evangelism into the rural areas, and nowhere was Kagawa more at home, despite his long life spent so much in the big towns.

Writer, pacifist, evangelist, social worker, reformer—what, then, was Kagawa's chief role? How does one match up against another of his activities? For what must he be mainly remembered?

He was, for a long time, a well-known name in the Christian Church all over the world; but he was not a world figure, certainly not in the sense that Schweitzer was one. He made no major contribution to the theological or philosophical thinking of his time, as did the German missionary. For some strange reason, the man who leaves home and goes to work in another country normally captures the imagination more than the one who stays at home, however important his work. When the World Council of Churches came into existence, after the Second World War, he was both too unwell and too much involved in his own country to travel far. Nor was he a man who really belonged to the councils of the Church. He was too busy to sit for long in offices or committees, and too practical to direct without doing at the same time. Even his writing was almost flung off like sparks from the work in which he was engaged.

These two things—his incessant activity and his consuming interest in the affairs of his own land—are the clearest pointers to his importance. When there is added to them the fact that the one story about him which really captured the imagination of the world was his immersion in the slums of Shinkawa, his real significance is evident.

William Temple once said that Christianity was the most materialistic of all religions. Kagawa, at the opposite side of the world, growing up amongst religions which taught subjection to fate and the acceptance of poverty and suffering as the rule of life, was early led to the same truth. He found the Protestant Church in Japan very reluctant to accept such a dictum, far more concerned with the maintenance of buildings and worship than with the needs of a depressed community. He gave himself to the service of those in need. But it was not as the result of an uneasy conscience about the poor that he did so. It was because he had seen Christ and had a vision of the Cross. It was because he had once prayed: 'Make me like Christ.' It was because, more than any man of his time in Japan, he was consumed by the compassion of Christ.

His true significance lies in the fact that he would not allow any divorce between worship and service, and used every means at his disposal, including that of an untiring personal example, to show that evangelism must be matched by compassion, that the Church and its members *must* work out their faith in their daily life, and that devotion to Christ must drive men and women, at whatever personal cost, to serve those in need.

The years passed. Other leaders arose in the Japanese Church. New links were forged with churches throughout the world. Schemes, organizations, advances came into being of which he had not dreamed and in which he had no share. But he was never a spent force. Japan would not have been merely a poorer place without him; it would hardly have been the same country. Not a few of the great changes which had taken place between the two great wars derived from his work and influence. In every part of the national life there were those who recognized this fact. They made it plain in the earlier part of 1959.

That year, Dr Toyohiko Kagawa was seventy. He had just published *The Purpose of the Universe*, a philosophical work on the nature of the world and God's plan for it. There gathered in Tokyo a great company, three hundred leaders from Christian, political, commercial, philanthropic and cultural circles, to celebrate his birthday and do him honour. Speeches were made with all the ceremony and courtesy natural to the Japanese people. The old man, deeply moved, his eyes so filled with tears that he could hardly see with his one semi-sighted eye, spoke quietly. It was difficult to hear what he said, but that scarcely mattered.

The only thing of importance was that he should know that he was greatly loved, that Japan honoured him as it honoured few of its sons.

When it was all over, when he had heard that it was proposed to make a film about his life and work, he made his way slowly home. He went into the simple, charming house. Now it was quiet, free from the busy chatter of the years. Here was the place where he had found security through the years. Here, too, was his devoted wife, the gracious woman who had shared his life from the days of the nine-by-six hut in Shinkawa nearly fifty years earlier. Here was peace.

They spoke of the day that was coming to an end, of the years they had shared, of Japan, the land they loved. There was still so much to be done. But now, others must carry the burden and enter into the joy of compassion. Others—and God. Always it was Christ who had really borne the burden, not Toyohiko himself. He prayed quietly. 'Take Thou the burden, Lord.' It was a prayer he had prayed before. In a sense he had prayed it from the moment he gave himself to Christ in Dr Harry Myers's room when he was fifteen years old.

> Take Thou the burden, Lord,
> I am exhausted with this heavy load.
> My tired hands tremble,
> And I stumble, stumble
> Along the way.
> O, lead me with Thine unfailing arm
> Again today.
>
> Unless Thou lead me, Lord,
> The road I journey on is all too hard.
> Through trust in Thee alone
> Can I go on.

Yet not for self alone
Thus do I groan;
My people's sorrows are the load I bear.
Lord, hear my prayer—
May Thy strong hand
Strike off all chains
That load my well-loved land.
God, draw her close to Thee.

The birthday celebration was the old man's last great public appearance. The years of illness, unremitting service and self-denial had begun to wear him down at last. Ever since the war ended he had been growing more obviously frail, and the attacks of pneumonia and bronchial trouble had come more often and lasted longer. Now, he could resist them no more. Not even his gallant spirit could drive the emaciated body into action again. He took to his bed, and seldom left it.

As long as he could, he dictated letters to his secretaries, but the time came when his wife had to deal with correspondence even with his more intimate friends. Some of them came to see him, from America and other countries, but as winter came and Christmas passed, he became too weak to talk with them, and in the shaded room his almost blind eyes could hardly recognize them.

A whole year of illness passed. He had never been so long inactive, and he waited peacefully for the end to come. Haru Kagawa, an old lady now, was constantly with him, and her voice recalled the days when he walked with 'Miss Spring' on the beach or escaped for brief hours from the slums of Shinkawa to climb the green slopes of Mount Rokko with her. The winter months went slowly by and the spring came to Japan once more. The blossoms were bursting and the countryside became a place of such loveliness as perhaps only Japan can fully show. People streamed into the church near by for the Easter services, and the joyous hymns of the Resurrection were echoed in the Kagawa house.

On 23rd April 1960, Toyohiko Kagawa died. No moment could have been more fitting for his passing. He had spent all his life trying to make his land a place of beauty, and to the end he walked with his Risen Lord.